ISSUES THAT CONCERN YOU

Medical Marijuana

Arthur Gillard, *Book Editor*

GREENHAVEN PRESS

A part of Gale, Cengage Learning

GALE
CENGAGE Learning·

Detroit • New York • San Francisco • New Haven, Conn • Waterville, Maine • London

Elizabeth Des Chenes, *Director, Content Strategy*
Cynthia Sanner, *Publisher*
Douglas Dentino, *Manager, New Product*

Articles in Greenhaven Press anthologies are often edited for length to meet page requirements. In addition, original titles of these works are changed to clearly present the main thesis and to explicitly indicate the author's opinion. Every effort is made to ensure that Greenhaven Press accurately reflects the original intent of the authors. Every effort has been made to trace the owners of copyrighted material.

Cover image © Andre Blais/Shutterstock.com.

LIBRARY OF CONGRESS CATALOGING-IN-PUBLICATION DATA

Medical marijuana / Arthur Gillard, book editor.
   pages cm. -- (Issues that concern you)
Audience: 14-18.
Audience: Grade 9 to 12.
Includes bibliographical references and index.
ISBN 978-0-7377-6297-6 (hardcover)
1. Marijuana--Therapeutic use--Juvenile literature. I. Gillard, Arthur.
RM666.C266M425 2013
615.3'2345--dc23

2013001149

Printed in the United States of America
1 2 3 4 5 6 7 17 16 15 14 13

CONTENTS

In the late 1970s, when Emily Gibson was a medical student, she had a friend who was dying from breast cancer that had spread throughout her body. When nothing else worked to treat the relentless nausea from chemotherapy treatment, her friend's doctor finally suggested that she might want to try marijuana. She complied, but found the way it altered her consciousness unpleasant and felt uncomfortable filling her house with marijuana smoke when she had a couple of teenage children living at home. Gibson, desperate to help her friend be comfortable enough to stay at home with her family in the final days of her life rather than continuing to spend so much of that time in the hospital, found a way to administer the marijuana in suppository form, which relieved her friend's nausea yet left her feeling much less "stoned." Although she was clearly breaking the law—this was almost twenty years before individual states started passing medical marijuana legislation—and could have gotten in a great deal of trouble for it, Gibson did what she felt she had to do to help her dying friend.

These days Gibson sees a darker side of marijuana. In her work treating people with addiction, she has come into contact with many people who use marijuana as a means of numbing themselves against and avoiding life, and as a worker in a medical clinic at a university, she has had a number of healthy young students ask her to give recommendations for medical marijuana, presumably so that they could use the drug recreationally without fear of getting arrested. She is particularly concerned about young people who use marijuana frequently—which she believes is more common due to a false belief that marijuana is completely safe—who she says are "so much less alive and engaged with the world." According to Gibson, for these problem users "it can mean more than temporary anesthesia to the unpleasantness of everyday hassles. They never really experience life in its full emotional range from joy to sadness, learning the sensitivity of becoming vulnerable, the lessons of experiencing discomfort and coping, and the healing balm of a resilient spirit. Instead, it is all about avoidance."[1]

Marijuana has been used as a medicine for thousands of years and was available legally in the United States in dozens of different medications prior to 1937, when the Marihuana Tax Act (*marihuana* was an alternative and now archaic spelling) ushered in the era of marijuana prohibition in the United States. To a large extent it was marijuana's controversial role as a recreational drug that led to it being banned in America and around the world in the first half of the twentieth century, and its central role in the countercultural movement of the 1960s greatly intensified the controversy that has raged around the plant ever since. As a

Seventy-three percent of Americans now believe that doctors should be able to prescribe medical marijuana, while public support for full legalization continues to grow as well.

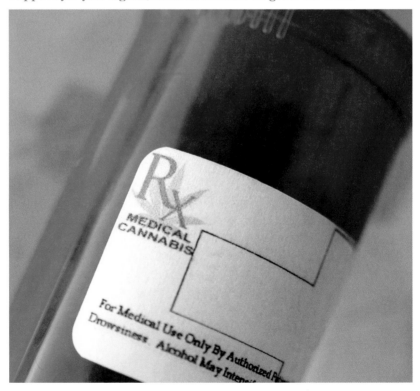

result, it has become difficult, if not impossible, to fully separate the medicinal properties of the plant from its role as a pleasure drug. Highly polarized positions have formed around the issue, with some arguing that it is a highly dangerous drug of abuse, addiction, even insanity, that must be stamped out at any cost— while others claim that it is both completely harmless and a miracle cure for almost every ill. In searching for the truth about such a controversial topic, one must be careful to discern the needles of truth buried in the haystacks of misinformation and propaganda. As David Nutt, chair of the Independent Scientific Committee on Drugs (www.drugscience.org.uk) and author of *Drugs Without the Hot Air: Minimising the Harms of Legal and Illegal Drugs*, points out, "Unfortunately, there's an awful lot of misinformation about drugs, both on the Internet and in the media. Any source that says 'all drugs are evil' or 'taking drugs is totally fine' is definitely not to be trusted!"[2] Although he was making his point about drugs in general, his comment certainly applies to marijuana, whether it is being considered as medication or recreation.

One of the conditions that many say medical marijuana is particularly helpful for is multiple sclerosis (MS), a disabling disease of the central nervous system characterized by a progressive loss of motor control. A patient with the disease describes how using marijuana vastly improved the quality of her life:

A few years ago I had started to eat small quantities of marijuana. . . . The effects were immediate and remarkable. Control of bladder functioning, which was a humiliating problem, is restored to normal and has been a liberating influence in my life-style. I can now go out shopping, to the theater, and various other places, without anticipation of dread and panic. Painful and disturbing attacks of spasticity are relieved and now restful patterns of sleep are ensured where previously sleep was disturbed by urinary frequency or pain and discomfort. Not least, I can laugh and giggle, have marvelous sex and forget that I have this awful, incurable, intractable disease.[3]

According to Julie Holland, a psychiatrist specializing in psychopharmacology (mind-altering drugs) and editor of *The Pot Book: A Complete Guide to Cannabis*, the benefits of medical marijuana for some patients may go beyond simply treating their symptoms or even—as some preliminary research suggests—directly treating a disease; e.g., by slowing the progression of MS or shrinking cancerous tumors. Holland suggests that "beyond the medical benefits of cannabis, one should not ignore the psychological and psychospiritual issues that are equally important. Using cannabis as an aid in relaxation, meditation, or just 'being' can be an important component of self-care. Many stress-reduction therapies in medicine focus on meditation and being present 'in the moment' as a basis of health and mindfulness. Too many of our vices rely on distraction and escape, numbing our minds and bodies, but cannabis is a drug that, better than most, facilitates being in the moment and being mindful."[4] Emily Gibson's remarks about how marijuana use can lead to numbness and disengagement contrast sharply with Holland's comments about the way it can help people become more mindful and engaged with the world, highlighting how deeply people disagree about the qualities of this complex psychoactive and medicinal plant.

A decisive majority of Americans now believe that doctors should be allowed to prescribe medical marijuana—73 percent hold that opinion, according to a *Reason*-Rupe poll conducted in September 2012. Support for full legalization (for recreational as well as medical use) continues to grow as well. In October 2011 the Gallup polling organization reported that support for marijuana legalization had reached 50 percent of the population for the first time; among those eighteen to twenty-nine years old, 62 percent were in favor of full legalization. In November 2012 two states—Colorado and Washington—made history by passing referendums making recreational marijuana use by adults legal under state law, though it remains illegal at the federal level.

As the momentum toward fully legalizing marijuana grows, is it possible that some clarity may begin to emerge in the contentious debate over marijuana's possible role as medicine? If, at some point in the future, marijuana becomes a legally accepted recreational drug throughout the United States, would that allow people to finally begin to separate the issues surrounding recreational use from its possible role as medicine? Or would that only intensify the conflict? Regardless of how this controversy shakes out in the long term, over the next few years or decades the possible role of marijuana in medicine and in society at large promises to continue to be a contentious issue.

Authors in this anthology offer a variety of perspectives on medical marijuana. In addition, the volume contains a thorough bibliography, a list of organizations to contact for further information, and appendixes to help the reader understand and explore the topic. The appendix titled "What You Should Know About Medical Marijuana" offers facts about the problem. The appendix "What You Should Do About Medical Marijuana" offers advice for young people who are concerned with this issue. With all these features, *Issues That Concern You: Medical Marijuana* provides an excellent resource for everyone interested in this timely, ongoing issue.

Notes

1. Emily Gibson, "The Unintended Consequences of Medical Marijuana," KevinMD.com, June 10, 2011. www.kevinmd .com/blog/2011/06/unintended-consequences-medical -marijuana.html.
2. David Nutt, *Drugs Without the Hot Air: Minimising the Harms of Legal and Illegal Drugs*. Cambridge: UIT Cambridge, 2012, p. 312.
3. Julie Holland, *The Pot Book: A Complete Guide to Cannabis; Its Role in Medicine, Politics, Science, and Culture*. Rochester, VT: Park Street, 2010, pp. 319–320.
4. Holland, *The Pot Book*, p. 246.

ONE

An Overview of Medical Marijuana

Heather M. Griffiths

Heather M. Griffiths has a PhD in philosophy from the University of Delaware and has worked as a survey administrator at the university's Center for Drug and Alcohol Studies. In the following viewpoint Griffiths notes that the use of marijuana for medical purposes is believed to have originated in China and had spread throughout much of the world by the first century AD, making its way to North America by the eighteenth century. Despite this widespread medical use, a morality movement in the United States led to marijuana's being prohibited for any purpose in 1937. According to the author, the current situation is complex, with some states allowing medical use of marijuana, while the federal government still considers any use of the drug to be illegal. In addition, some pharmaceutical medications consisting of active components of marijuana ("cannabinoids") in pure form are currently available by prescription, though there is controversy over whether they are as effective as smoked marijuana.

Heather M. Griffiths, "Medical Use of Marijuana," *Encyclopedia of Substance Abuse Prevention, Treatment, & Recovery*, vol. 1, Gary L. Fisher and Nancy A. Roget, eds. Sage Publications, 2009, pp. 529–532. Copyright © 2009 by SAGE Publications. All rights reserved. Reproduced by permission.

Medical marijuana (*cannabis sativa*) refers to the medically controlled use of marijuana or tetrahydrocannabinol (THC, the main psychoactive ingredient in marijuana) by patients seeking a means to address medical problems including nausea, vomiting, weight loss, multiple sclerosis, asthma, inflammation, glaucoma, poor appetite, spasticity, chronic pain, and acute pain. There is a consensus that marijuana's medical use developed first in China, spreading to India, Rome, and Greece by the 1st century and eventually reaching Europe and Africa. The use of marijuana as medicine finally spread to the European colonies in North America sometime in the 18th century.

Thus, the use of medically controlled marijuana in the United States predates the 1937 Marihuana Tax Act [the name reflects an older spelling], which rendered cannabis illegal even with a physician's prescription. Moral crusades condemning the use of marijuana for any purpose prior to the 1937 Marihuana Tax Act and widespread illegal use of marijuana since the passage of that law contributes to the contemporary controversy over developing clinical studies to assess the efficacy of medical treatments using marijuana. Although a few states did enact legislation (primarily in the 1970s and 1980s) that allows physicians to prescribe marijuana, federal law prohibiting this practice prevents physicians from prescribing marijuana as medication. Currently [as of 2012], the federal government of the United States does not recognize marijuana as serving any legitimate medical function. However, some synthetic cannabinoids [chemicals such as THC and related substances found in marijuana that affect cannabinoid receptors in the body, causing physical and/or psychoactive effects], for example, dronabinol, fall into the Schedule III drug category [drugs that have an accepted medical use and relatively low abuse potential]. These synthetic cannabinoids mimic some of marijuana's medical effects while costing considerably more. However, because they have a standardized dosage, regulators consider these to have a low potential for abuse.

The contemporary debate over medical marijuana consists of two opposing arguments. One side of the debate suggests that medical marijuana is unnecessary because existing drugs address

A scientist extracts THC from marijuana for medical use. THC is the main psychoactive ingredient in marijuana.

all conditions that medical marijuana may ameliorate. Opponents suggest that medical marijuana is more effective and less expensive than existing legal drugs. Although in the United States medical marijuana legislation is limited to compassionate use laws in approximately 13 states [many more have been added since this writing], global legislation (and attitudes) toward both marijuana and medical marijuana vary greatly, and there is a social movement industry centered around marijuana use, particularly decriminalizing-legalizing the medical use of marijuana.

Contemporary Debate

Many studies conducted in the 1970s, some of which resulted in follow-up studies in the 1980s and 1990s, confirm that cannabinoid drugs are effective in treating appetite loss, glaucoma, nausea and vomiting, pain, spasticity, and weight loss. Opponents of decriminalizing-legalizing marijuana for medical use contend that legal drugs, such as dronabinol, alleviate medical conditions as efficiently as marijuana. To this argument, supporters of medical marijuana reply that the presence of an existing treatment does not preclude developing and approving alternative treatments. For example, there is more than one drug therapy approved for the treatment of depression and more than one kind of pain medication. In addition, the legal cannabinoid drug dronabinol, which mimics the effect of marijuana, has more side effects than inhaled marijuana, costs more, takes longer for a patient to experience the beneficial effects, and presents ingestion difficulty for both vomiting patients and patients whose symptoms include throat swelling. It is also far easier for patients to control their dosage of inhaled marijuana because they can monitor their body's reactions and cease inhaling when undesirable side effects present themselves, an advantage that cannot be obtained with a dosage-standardized pill.

Almost 40 years ago, tests demonstrated that inhaled marijuana was effective in treating glaucoma by lowering pressure within the eye, thus protecting the patient from damage to the optic nerve. However, alternative treatments developed in the late 1990s are equally efficacious in safeguarding the optic nerve. Additionally, The American Academy of Ophthalmology does not promote marijuana as a safe or effective treatment for glaucoma because while marijuana may reduce intraocular pressure, at the high dosage required to treat glaucoma (8–10 [joints] per day) undesirable side effects appear.

Further research on using medical marijuana to treat glaucoma is unlikely. Though studies show that it is an effective means of reducing intraocular pressure, existing treatments protect the optic nerve as effectively without the numerous side effects of a therapeutic dosage of marijuana. However, professional organizations such as The American Academy of Ophthalmology and The National Eye Institute, while not currently endorsing medical marijuana as a glaucoma treatment, state their willingness to reconsider this position following further research.

Using Marijuana for Pain Management

Although case studies testing the effectiveness of inhaled marijuana on both specific and general pain, including pain induced by surgical intervention, headache, and chronic illness do exist, it is difficult to separate the actual effect of inhaled or ingested marijuana on physical pain from the expectation that inhaled marijuana produces a pain-relieving effect (the placebo effect).

Conclusions drawn from large-scale studies assessing the effectiveness of marijuana on acute pain are mixed. In one 1977 study, most respondents preferred a presurgical intervention of diazepam (antianxiety medication) or a placebo to intravenous THC prior to tooth extraction. However, at least one controlled experiment conducted in 1974 using more reliable measures of pain tolerance indicate that higher doses of THC may reduce acute pain.

One 1975 study regarding the efficacy of marijuana for treating chronic pain resulting from cancer demonstrated that chronic pain caused by cancer responds to high doses of oral THC (20 mg) and high doses of codeine (120 mg) comparably. However, researchers also concluded that the negative side effects of high-dosage oral THC were more negative than that of high-dosage codeine, including anxiety, paranoia, dizziness, and depression. However, this study utilized oral, rather than inhaled doses, which affects several factors related to the efficacy of treatment, including strength and absorption of the drug. Although it is true that the use of marijuana induces side effects, not all patients experience these effects, and indeed, some patients may prefer the side effects of marijuana use to the pain cancer causes.

In addition to treating chronic pain resulting from cancer, numerous studies demonstrate that both orally ingested and inhaled marijuana is effective in treating nausea and vomiting related to cancer treatments. Studies also demonstrated that the synthetic cannabinoids nabilone and levonantradol reduced nausea and vomiting when taken prior to treatment. The differing anti-emetic [anti-nausea/vomiting] effects of inhaled marijuana, ingested marijuana, and synthetic cannabinoids warrants further research because inhaled marijuana is more cost-effective, offers patients more control over dosage, and serves as an additional drug with which to rotate patients developing tolerance to existing anti-emetics. Additionally, because medicines vary in their impact on the individual, some patients may find inhaled marijuana more effective than standard antinausea drugs. Although it is true that medically controlled marijuana does present side effects, patients may prefer these side effects to chemotherapy-induced nausea.

US Legislation

The 1970 Comprehensive Drug Abuse Prevention and Control Act divided substances into categories based on their medical use and potential for addiction. Marijuana, along with heroin, mescaline, and lysergic acid diethylamide (LSD), is a Schedule I drug, meaning that the Drug Enforcement Administration legally classifies marijuana and cannabis as (a) carrying a high potential for abuse, (b) without currently accepted medical use in the United States, and/or (c) lacking accepted safe use even with medical supervision. Even with this classification, for a brief period, the federal government allowed citizens to apply for relief from this law as part of a compassionate use program. A compassionate use exception would allow collection of data regarding the efficacy of medical marijuana; however, the federal government discontinued compassionate use exceptions in 1992 despite the increasing number of people who applied for it every year.

Since marijuana is a Schedule I drug, physicians cannot legally prescribe it, and possession of the drug can lead to large fines and/or jail time. However, the use of medical marijuana outside the United States, state legislation related to medical marijuana developed over the past 10 years, and contemporary efforts to reschedule marijuana to allow medical use provides evidence for the conflicting attitudes that characterize the current climate toward medical marijuana.

California's 1996 Compassionate Use Act (Proposition 215) states that a seriously ill Californian may use marijuana with a physician's recommendation that the patient might benefit from its use. Since 2000, legislators in Hawaii, Vermont, and Rhode Island have passed bills protecting seriously ill patients from prosecution for using marijuana as medicine. In 2007, New Mexico's legislators passed a law giving the state Department of Health a mandate to develop rules for the use and distribution of medical marijuana to patients authorized by the state. These are only some of the examples of state laws regarding medical marijuana.

A ruling in *Conant v. Walters* in 2002 found that federal authorities could not legally sanction physicians for frankly discussing medical marijuana with patients. Although the holding did not affect physicians' inability to prescribe medical marijuana, it did affirm that physicians could legally endorse or recommend the use of marijuana to patients.

Social Movements, Global Attitudes

National and international social movement organizations supporting the decriminalization or legalization of marijuana, particularly medical marijuana, continue to thrive. These social movement organizations include the Drug Policy Foundation and the Drug Policy Alliance operating in the United States, The National Organization for the Reform of Marijuana Laws operating in the United Kingdom and the United States, the European Movement for the Normalization of Drug Policy, and the International Anti-Prohibition League.

Drug laws in Western Europe vary widely from country to country. Today [2009], in some European countries, it is a criminal offense to use medical marijuana; in some, it is a civil matter; and in a few, marijuana is completely decriminalized. Most recent legislation demonstrates a trend of moving away from harsh penalties for marijuana use and toward a harm reduction model that would allow more patients to access marijuana for medical use. In 2003, the Netherlands, continuing its trend of liberal drug policy

States That Have Passed Medical Marijuana Legislation (as of September 2012)

Seventeen states and the District of Columbia have legalized medical marijuana as of September 2012. The rules under which medical marijuana is available vary widely from state to state.

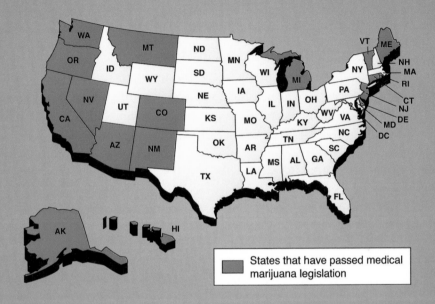

States that have passed medical marijuana legislation

Note: Based on data from the Marijuana Policy Project.

Taken from: Heesun Wee. "Momentum Swinging Against Medical Marijuana." *CNBC*, April 19, 2012. www.cnbc.com.

and legislation, became the first country to enact federal regulations that allowed pharmacies to distribute medical cannabis.

In recent years, the United Kingdom moved toward harm reduction policies in its drug laws. Marijuana is decriminalized and simple possession does not result in arrest. However, in the United Kingdom, medical marijuana is not legal. This policy means that even patients using marijuana to address medical conditions are subject to verbal warnings and the confiscation of the drug. In Canada, patients may use medical marijuana if

(a) they suffer from serious illness, (b) existing treatments do not provide relief for either the illness or symptoms related to treatment of the illness, and (c) the benefits offered to the patients outweigh the risks posed by use of marijuana. Mexico's drug laws are similar to [those of] the United States, and Mexico does not currently [2009] have any laws decriminalizing or legalizing medical marijuana.

The Controversy Continues

Proponents of medical marijuana focus on the benefit of inhaling smoke rather than on ingesting pills when treating patients with nausea, as well as on the importance of developing medical alternatives for patients who fail to respond to conventional drug therapy. Current federal legislation in the United States creates difficulty for large-scale assessment of medical marijuana's effectiveness as a treatment, though older studies (primarily from the 1970s) confirm the efficacy of cannabinoids for treating a variety of maladies. Contemporaneously, following California's 1996 Proposition 215, several states enacted compassionate use laws that allow patients to use marijuana with a physician's recommendation without legal penalty. Opponents of legalizing and/or decriminalizing marijuana for medical purposes [believe] that existing drugs offer sufficient treatment for all medical conditions that may respond to marijuana, as well as argue that marijuana causes harmful physiological effects. Both the potential medical benefits and negative side effects created by medically controlled marijuana warrant further research.

TWO

Medical Marijuana Has Numerous Medical Benefits

Steve Fox, Paul Armentano, and Mason Tvert

Steve Fox is the director of state campaigns for the Marijuana Policy Project (MPP) and cofounder of Safer Alternative for Enjoyable Recreation (SAFER). Paul Armentano is the deputy director of NORML (The National Organization for the Reform of Marijuana Laws) and the 2008 recipient of the Project Censored Real News Award for Outstanding Investigative journalism. Mason Tvert is the cofounder and executive director of SAFER. In the following viewpoint Fox, Armentano, and Tvert argue that marijuana effectively relieves symptoms of disease; for example, reducing pain, inflammation, muscle spasms and incontinence. They also claim that cannabis can treat disease directly. For example, they cite studies showing that chemical constituents of marijuana called cannabinoids can cause cancer tumors to shrink and other studies suggesting marijuana may prevent diabetes and slow the progress of multiple sclerosis. The authors discuss the case of Cathy Jordan, a medical marijuana patient afflicted with a neurodegenerative disease who has lived much longer than expected.

Cannabis possesses a variety of therapeutic applications. Most of you reading this are undoubtedly familiar with some of the ways that marijuana can provide symptomatic relief. After all, pot's prowess as an appetite stimulant has been a source of late-night comedy sketches for decades now. (Yes, smoking marijuana will give you "the munchies." Of course, if you're suffering from severe weight loss due to HIV, AIDS, cancer chemotherapy, or cachexia [rapid weight loss due to chronic illness], the munchies is a life-saving side effect—not a laughing matter.) You are also likely aware of the use of cannabis to treat severe nausea—inhaling pot reduces the "gag reflex"—and glaucoma, an eye disorder characterized by abnormally high pressure within the eyeball. (Smoking marijuana temporarily reduces intraocular ["inside the eye"] pressure.) And we're pretty sure all of you know that marijuana can elevate mood and alleviate anxiety.

Some of you may have also heard that cannabis can reduce involuntary muscle spasms and incontinence, symptoms commonly associated with multiple sclerosis and other movement disorders. Marijuana can also induce sleep, alleviate the tics associated with Tourette's syndrome, and significantly reduce inflammation and pain, particularly neuropathy (a type of nerve pain that's notoriously difficult to treat with standard analgesics [pain killers]). A 2007 study conducted at San Francisco General Hospital concluded that smoking cannabis reduced HIV-associated sensory neuropathy in patients by more than 30 percent. "Smoked cannabis was well tolerated and effectively relieved chronic neuropathic pain from HIV-associated neuropathy," scientists reported in the journal *Neurology*.

Beyond Symptomatic Relief

Chances are that far fewer of you are aware that cannabis's medical utility extends far beyond treating just the symptoms of disease. In some cases, it appears that marijuana can effectively treat disease itself. For instance, marijuana possesses strong antioxidant properties that can protect the brain during trauma and potentially ward off the onset of certain neurological diseases such as

Therapeutic Effects of Marijuana

Therapeutic Effects	Therapeutic Use
Bronchodilation	Bronchial asthma
Antiemetic effect	Prevention of nausea/vomiting caused by anticancer drugs
Appetite stimulation	Palliative care for anorexia caused by opioids, antiviral drugs, AIDS-related illnesses or terminal cancer
Analgesia	Cancer pain, post–operative pain, phantom limb pain
Decreased spasticity/ataxia/ muscle weakness	Multiple sclerosis, cerebral palsy, spinal cord injuries
Decreased intraocular pressure	Glaucoma

Taken from: "Therapeutic Effects of Cannabis." Lundbeck Institute CNSforum. www.cnsforum.com.

Alzheimers. In fact, in one of the great political ironies, the U.S. Department of Health and Human Services holds a patent—it's patent no. 6630507—on the use of cannabinoids as antioxidants and neuroprotectants. That's right, the same government that classifies cannabis as a Schedule I illicit drug (which under federal law is defined as possessing "no currently accepted medical use in treatment") owns the intellectual property rights to several of the plant's naturally occurring, therapeutic chemicals!

The long-term use of cannabinoids appears to slow the progression of certain neurological and autoimmune diseases such as multiple sclerosis [MS]. In clinical trials, MS patients taking Sativex (an oral spray consisting of natural, whole-plant cannabis extracts) for a period of several years report requiring *fewer* daily doses of the drug to effectively treat their pain and spasticity. Because multiple sclerosis is a progressive disease, conventional wisdom dictates that patients should be taking more doses, not fewer, over time to attain the same relief. Writing in the journal *Brain*, British researchers concluded, "Cannabis may also slow

Marijuana has been found to be effective as an appetite stimulant for patients with HIV/AIDS and cachexia, as well as those undergoing chemotherapy for cancer.

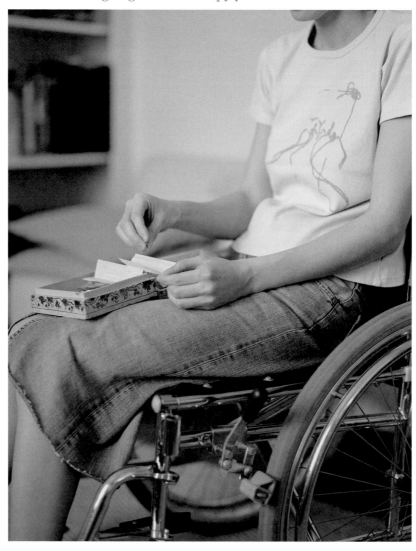

the neurodegenerative processes that ultimately lead to chronic disability in multiple sclerosis and probably other diseases."

A Medical Marijuana Success Story

Preclinical reports also indicate that cannabis may moderate the progression of amyotrophic lateral sclerosis (a.k.a. Lou Gehrig's Disease [or ALS]), a fatal neurodegenerative disorder, and at least one study demonstrated that the administration of THC [tetra-hydrocannabinol, the main psychoactive ingredient of marijuana] both before and after the onset of ALS halted disease progression and prolonged survival in mice. Would pot have this same effect in humans? For that answer, all one has to do is ask Cathy Jordan. . . .

Cathy has lived with ALS longer than almost anyone in America—an accomplishment she credits almost entirely to her use of cannabis. Diagnosed with the disease in 1986, Cathy was given only years to live (more than half of ALS patients die within three years after the onset of symptoms). Between 1986 and 1989, doctors prescribed Cathy a steady stream of muscle relaxants and mood-altering narcotics. Despite her steady diet of pharmaceuticals, neither Cathy's condition nor her mood improved. By the late 1980s, she became despondent and wanted to die. And then a friend suggested she try cannabis.

The therapeutic effects of Cathy's first marijuana cigarette were both immediate and profound. Cannabis dramatically alleviated her pain and relaxed her muscles, while simultaneously stimulating her appetite and elevating her mood. Within years Cathy had abandoned virtually all of her conventional medications in favor of cannabis, and her doctors—as well as those of us who know her—have been stunned by the results. "It's exciting to see the doctors pass out," she joked to a Florida newspaper in 2008. "They're just miffed that I'm so healthy."

Antitumor Effects

Finally studies have also shown that cannabinoids [chemicals such as THC and related substances found in marijuana that affect cannabinoid receptors in the body, causing physical and/

or psychoactive effects] can prevent the onset of diabetes and can limit the spread of multidrug-resistant infections such as MRSA [methicillin-resistant Staphylococcus aureus], more commonly known as "the Superbug." (According to the *Journal of the American Medical Association*, MRSA is responsible for nearly 20,000 hospital-stay-related deaths annually.) Marijuana also has profound cancer-fighting abilities. In laboratory settings, the controlled administration of cannabinoids selectively targets and kills malignant cancer cells associated with gliomas (brain cancer), prostate cancer, breast cancer, lung cancer, skin cancer, pancreatic cancer, and lymphoma. Writing in the prestigious journal *Nature*, Spanish researcher Manuel Guzman reported: "Cannabinoids inhibit tumor growth in laboratory animals. They do so by modulating key cell-signaling pathways, thereby inducing direct growth arrest and death of tumor cells, as well as by inhibiting tumor angiogenesis [creation of blood vessels] and metastasis [spread]. Cannabinoids are selective antitumor compounds, as they can kill tumor cells without affecting their non-transformed counterparts." Troublingly, a review of the scientific literature reveals that U.S. investigators first reported on the prolific anticancer properties of cannabis more than thirty years ago—in 1974! Yet to date, the U.S. government has never commissioned one single follow-up study assessing the potential of cannabis to treat this deadly disease.

THREE

Marijuana Has No Medicinal Value

US Drug Enforcement Administration

The US Drug Enforcement Administration (DEA) is a federal agency tasked with enforcing the controlled substances laws and regulations of the United States and reducing the availability of illicit controlled substances. In the following viewpoint taken from the January 2011 report *The DEA Position on Marijuana*, the authors argue that while some isolated chemical constituents of marijuana known as cannabinoids may have some medical utility, the form of marijuana available in some states for allegedly medical purposes is a dangerous drug with no medical utility. The authors note that modern medicine must meet strict criteria such as standardized dosage, quality control, and proof of medical effectiveness and that marijuana does not meet any of these criteria and therefore cannot be considered valid medicine. The DEA report quotes numerous official bodies, such as the American Medical Association, the American Cancer Society, and the British Medical Association, all of which oppose medical use of marijuana.

"The Fallacy of Marijuana for Medicinal Use: Smoked Marijuana Is Not Medicine," United States Department of Justice (USDOJ), January 2011, pp. 3–6.

In 1970, Congress enacted laws against marijuana based in part on its conclusion that marijuana has no scientifically proven medical value. Likewise, the Food and Drug Administration (FDA), which is responsible for approving drugs as safe and effective medicine, has thus far declined to approve smoked marijuana for any condition or disease. Indeed, the FDA has noted that "there is currently sound evidence that smoked marijuana is harmful," and "that no sound scientific studies support medical use of marijuana for treatment in the United States, and no animal or human data support the safety or efficacy of marijuana for general medical use."

The United States Supreme Court has also declined to carve out an exception for marijuana under a theory of medical viability. In 2001, for example, the Supreme Court decided that a 'medical necessity' defense against prosecution was unavailable to defendants because Congress had purposely placed marijuana into Schedule I, which enumerates those controlled substances without any medical benefits. . . .

In *Gonzales v. Raich* . . . the Court had another opportunity to create a type of 'medical necessity' defense in a case involving severely ill California residents who had received physician approval to cultivate and use marijuana under California's Compassionate Use Act (CUA). . . . Despite the state's attempt to shield its residents from liability under CUA, the Supreme Court held that Congress' power to regulate interstate drug markets included the authority to regulate wholly intrastate markets as well. Consequently, the Court again declined to carve out a 'medical necessity' defense, finding that the CSA [the Controlled Substances Act] was not diminished in the face of any state law to the contrary and could support the specific enforcement actions at issue.

In a show of support for the *Raich* decision, the International Narcotics Control Board (INCB) issued this statement urging other countries to consider the real dangers of cannabis:

Cannabis is classified under international conventions as a drug with a number of personal and public health problems.

It is not a 'soft' drug as some people would have you believe. There is new evidence confirming well-known mental health problems, and some countries with a more liberal policy towards cannabis are reviewing their position. Countries need to take a strong stance towards cannabis abuse.

Widespread Opposition to Medical Marijuana in the Medical Community

The DEA [Drug Enforcement Administration] and the federal government are not alone in viewing smoked marijuana as having no documented medical value. Voices in the medical community likewise do not accept smoked marijuana as medicine:

- The American Medical Association (AMA) has always endorsed "well-controlled studies of marijuana and related cannabinoids [chemicals found in marijuana that have physical and/or psychoactive effects] in patients with serious conditions for which preclinical, anecdotal, or controlled evidence suggests possible efficacy and the application of such results to the understanding and treatment of disease." In November 2009, the AMA amended its policy, urging that marijuana's status as a Schedule I controlled substance be reviewed "with the goal of facilitating the conduct of clinical research and development of cannabinoid-based medicines, and alternate delivery methods." The AMA also stated that "this should not be viewed as an endorsement of state-based medical cannabis programs, the legalization of marijuana, or that scientific evidence on the therapeutic use of cannabis meets the current standards for prescription drug product."
- The American Society of Addiction Medicine's (ASAM) public policy statement on "Medical Marijuana," clearly rejects smoking as a means of drug delivery. ASAM further recommends that "all cannabis, cannabis-based products and cannabis delivery devices should be subject to the same standards applicable to all other prescription medication and

medical devices, and should not be distributed or otherwise provided to patients . . ." without FDA approval. ASAM also "discourages state interference in the federal medication approval process."

- The American Cancer Society (ACS) "does not advocate inhaling smoke, nor the legalization of marijuana," although the organization does support carefully controlled clinical studies for alternative delivery methods, specifically a tetra-hydrocannabinol (THC) skin patch.
- The American Glaucoma Society (AGS) has stated that "although marijuana can lower the intraocular pressure, the side effects and short duration of action, coupled with the lack of evidence that its use alters the course of glaucoma, preclude recommending this drug in any form for the treatment of glaucoma at the present time."
- The American Academy of Pediatrics (AAP) believes that "[a]ny change in the legal status of marijuana, even if limited to adults, could affect the prevalence of use among adolescents." While it supports scientific research on the possible medical use of cannabinoids as opposed to smoked marijuana, it opposes the legalization of marijuana.
- The National Multiple Sclerosis Society (NMSS) has stated that it could not recommend medical marijuana be made widely available for people with multiple sclerosis for symptom management, explaining: "This decision was not only based on existing legal barriers to its use but, even more importantly, because studies to date do not demonstrate a clear benefit compared to existing symptomatic therapies and because side effects, systemic effects, and long-term effects are not yet clear."
- The British Medical Association (BMA) voiced extreme concern that downgrading the criminal status of marijuana would "mislead" the public into believing that the drug is safe. The BMA maintains that marijuana "has been linked to greater risk of heart disease, lung cancer, bronchitis and emphysema." The 2004 Deputy Chairman of the BMA's Board of Science said that "[t]he public must be made aware of the harmful effects we know result from smoking this drug."

Although states have passed laws legalizing medical marijuana, the US Drug Enforcement Administration holds that marijuana has no medicinal value.

A Landmark Study

In 1999, The Institute of Medicine (IOM) released a landmark study reviewing the supposed medical properties of marijuana. The study is frequently cited by "medical" marijuana advocates, but in fact severely undermines their arguments.

- After release of the IOM study, the principal investigators cautioned that the active compounds in marijuana [cannabinoids] may have medicinal potential and therefore should be researched further. However, the study concluded that "there is little future in smoked marijuana as a medically approved medication."

- For some ailments, the IOM found ". . . potential therapeutic value of cannabinoid drugs, primarily THC, for pain relief, control of nausea and vomiting, and appetite stimulation." However, it pointed out that "[t]he effects of cannabinoids on the symptoms studied are generally modest, and in most cases there are more effective medications [than smoked marijuana]."
- The study concluded that, at best, there is only anecdotal information on the medical benefits of smoked marijuana for some ailments, such as muscle spasticity. For other ailments, such as epilepsy and glaucoma, the study found no evidence of medical value and did not endorse further research.
- The IOM study explained that "smoked marijuana . . . is a crude THC delivery system that also delivers harmful substances." In addition, "plants contain a variable mixture of biologically active compounds and cannot be expected to provide a precisely defined drug effect." Therefore, the study concluded that "there is little future in smoked marijuana as a medically approved medication."
- The principal investigators explicitly stated that using smoked marijuana in clinical trials "should not be designed to develop it as a licensed drug, but should be a stepping stone to the development of new, safe delivery systems of cannabinoids."

Thus, even scientists and researchers who believe that certain active ingredients in marijuana may have potential medicinal value openly *discount the notion that smoked marijuana is or can become "medicine."*

Smoked Marijuana Is Harmful

The Drug Enforcement Administration supports ongoing research into potential medicinal uses of marijuana's active ingredients. As of December 2010:

- There are 111 researchers registered with DEA to perform studies with marijuana, marijuana extracts, and non-tetrahydrocannabinol marijuana derivatives that exist in the plant, such as cannabidiol and cannabinol.

- Studies include evaluation of abuse potential, physical/psychological effects, adverse effects, therapeutic potential, and detection.
- Fourteen of the researchers are approved to conduct research with smoked marijuana on human subjects.

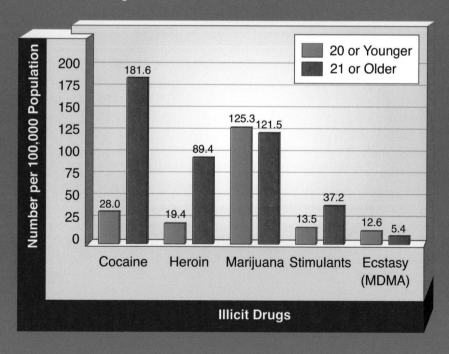

Emergency Department Visits Involving Major Illicit Drugs, by Age and Drug: 2009

In 2009, 376,467 emergency department (ED) visits involved marijuana use, making it the second-most common illicit drug involved in ED visits. For those under age 21, it is the most common illicit drug involved in ED visits.

At present, however, *the clear weight of the evidence is that smoked marijuana is harmful*. No matter what medical condition has been studied, other drugs already approved by the FDA have been proven to be safer than smoked marijuana.

The only drug currently approved by the FDA that contains the synthetic form of THC is Marinol®. Available through prescription, Marinol® comes in pill form, and is used to relieve nausea and vomiting associated with chemotherapy for cancer patients and to assist with loss of appetite with AIDS patients.

Sativex®, an oromucosal [inside the mouth] spray for the treatment of spasticity due to Multiple Sclerosis is already approved for use in Canada and was approved in June 2010 for use in the United Kingdom. The oral liquid spray contains two of the cannabinoids found in marijuana—THC and cannabidiol (CBD)—but unlike smoked marijuana, removes contaminants, reduces the intoxicating effects, is grown in a structured and scientific environment, administers a set dosage and meets criteria for pharmaceutical products.

"Medical" Marijuana Lacks Quality, Safety, and Efficacy

Organizers behind the "medical" marijuana movement have not dealt with ensuring that the product meets the standards of modern medicine: quality, safety and efficacy. There is no standardized composition or dosage; no appropriate prescribing information; no quality control; no accountability for the product; no safety regulation; no way to measure its effectiveness (besides anecdotal stories); and no insurance coverage. Science, not popular vote, should determine what medicine is.

The legalization movement is not simply a harmless academic exercise. The mortal danger of thinking that marijuana is "medicine" was graphically illustrated by a story from California. In the spring of 2004, Irma Perez was "in the throes of her first experience with the drug Ecstasy . . . when, after taking one Ecstasy tablet, she became ill and told friends that she felt like she was

. . . 'going to die.'. . . Two teenage acquaintances did not seek medical care and instead tried to get Perez to smoke marijuana. When that failed due to her seizures, the friends tried to force-feed marijuana leaves to her, "apparently because [they] knew that drug is sometimes used to treat cancer patients." Irma Perez lost consciousness and died a few days later when she was taken off life support. She was 14 years old.

FOUR

Teenagers Should Be Allowed to Use Marijuana for Medical Purposes

Andrew Myers

Andrew Myers is codirector of the Arizona Medical Marijuana Association. In the following viewpoint Myers argues that it is appropriate to allow minors (i.e., those under the age of full legal responsibility) to use marijuana for medical purposes when appropriate. According to the author, this would apply to only a very small number of young people with serious illnesses such as cancer, not, say, teens with minor injuries. He claims that the process by which a teenager would be determined eligible to use medical marijuana is quite stringent, much more so than with pharmaceutical narcotics; furthermore, narcotics that are commonly prescribed for minors are much more dangerous than medical marijuana. Myers argues that there is no reason to deny an alternative medical treatment such as marijuana to a patient in need, solely on the basis of the age of that patient.

It's important that we all understand how noncontroversial medical marijuana use by serious and terminally ill minor patients [under the age of full legal responsibility] is.

First, let's be clear who we are talking about. This is not about a 16-year-old with a skateboarding injury, which is how this issue is irresponsibly framed by those who have little interest in effective public health policy, and are more interested in playing politics than treating patients.

This is about providing a safe and effective treatment alternative for a very small group of minors who have very serious or even terminal illnesses like leukemia.

For patients who wish to avoid smoking, medical marijuana is available in many other forms, such as the baked goods, candies, and beverage shown here.

A Safe and Effective Medicine

We know, based on university research, that marijuana is a very safe and effective medication for treating nausea and wasting in cancer patients. If not treated effectively, these conditions often interrupt patients' treatment schedules, putting their lives at risk. In fact, many patients who fail on the entire range of traditionally prescribed anti-nausea medications find far greater relief with the use of marijuana with far fewer side effects. These improvements can be life-saving.

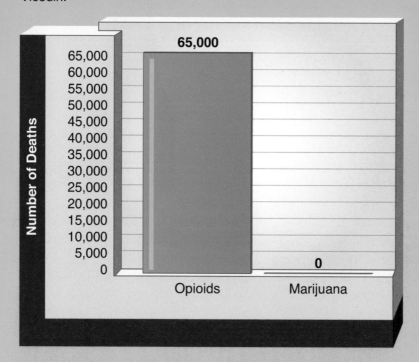

Overdose Deaths Due to Opioids and Marijuana, 1996–2006

Medical marijuana is much safer than many commonly used prescription medications, including synthetic opioids such as Vicodin.

For us to prohibit young cancer patients from accessing a potentially life-saving treatment for no other reason than their age would be unconscionable. Especially when almost all of the minor patients who would benefit from the law are already taking prescription medications that have a far greater risk of addiction and devastating side effects.

Narcotics are prescribed to minors on a regular basis. In fact, I myself was prescribed Vicodin twice for extended periods after reconstructive knee surgery when I was a minor. There was no controversy surrounding this treatment decision by my physician, even though—as any pharmacologist will tell you—Vicodin is a far more dangerous substance than marijuana.

Additionally, in the case of medical marijuana, two physicians must agree on the recommendation, and, of course, there must be parental permission given. This level of protection does not exist for the prescription of far more dangerous narcotic drugs. You can also be sure that the [Arizona] Department of Heath Services and the Medical Board will be paying close attention to marijuana recommendations for minor patients.

An Essential Treatment for Some Young Patients

Also important to remember is that, as a rule, these patients will not be smoking marijuana, but rather using other ingestion methods such as infused edibles (like cookies or yogurt) and tincture. These methods allow the patient to get the therapeutic benefits of the substance, without the danger and stigma of smoking.

Medical marijuana is potentially life-saving for some young cancer patients. There is absolutely no reason to exclude patients from a viable treatment alternative simply because of their age. This is a doctor-recommended medication that will be distributed by state-regulated facilities, not an illegal street drug. The protections in place are far more extensive than exist for more dangerous prescription drugs that are given freely to young people every day.

Don't be fooled by the scare tactics. Medical marijuana use by minors should be exceedingly rare, but for some patients, it is an essential treatment option, and one that will save lives.

FIVE

Medical Marijuana Increases Recreational Use by Teenagers

Kevin A. Sabet

Kevin A. Sabet is a fellow at the Center for Substance Abuse Solutions at the University of Pennsylvania and served as senior adviser to the White House Office of National Drug Control Policy (ONDCP) from 2009 to 2011. In the following viewpoint Sabet argues that the medical marijuana movement is causing increased recreational use by teenagers. The author refutes studies purportedly showing no increase in use in medical marijuana states, saying those studies had faulty methodology. According to Sabet, a more reliable study showed that states with medical marijuana legislation had nearly twice the rate of marijuana dependence and abuse as those without such legislation. He says surveys of teen drug use have found a decrease in social disapproval of marijuana smoking since 2007, along with a significant increase in use among teens. Sabet attributes this change to the medical marijuana movement's leading young people to perceive marijuana to be less harmful than it is.

Exactly two weeks to the day I was born in 1979, Keith Stroup, the head of the National Organization [for the Reform] of Marijuana Laws (NORML), told the Emory University school newspaper, *The Emory Wheel*, that "We are trying to get marijuana reclassified medically. If we do that, (we'll do it in at least 20 states this year for chemotherapy patients) we'll be using the issue as a red herring to give marijuana a good name."

So it is no surprise that last week, NORML—the nation's oldest marijuana legalization organization—published in their weekly newsletter the sweeping assertion that "medical marijuana has no discernible impact on marijuana use." NORML cited a new article in the *Annals of Epidemiology* (a respected publication to be sure; a similar epidemiology journal will soon release a study showing that marijuana is significantly linked with car crashes) which critiques an earlier article by [Melanie] Wall and colleagues showing an increase in marijuana use among states with medical marijuana. Essentially, the authors replicated the Wall study using different methods and got different results.

Increased Recreational Use in Medical Marijuana States

Certainly medical marijuana is a complex issue—one where politics, compassion, ethics and science collide. Sixteen states and D.C. [District of Columbia] technically have laws allowing marijuana as medicine on the books, but these laws, like other drug laws, vary widely in implementation, so it is tough to even perform studies linking medical marijuana with use changes. NORML doesn't seem too bothered by that. They went on to cite a Brown University study looking at Rhode Island—a state with a barely discernible medical marijuana program in the first place—as further "proof" that medical marijuana doesn't impact use. And the usual folks, like *Reason Online*, essentially republished the NORML line without any critical analysis.

A closer look at these studies shows something a little different, and much more nuanced. First, they completely ignore the more thorough studies that in fact do show increases in use. A major

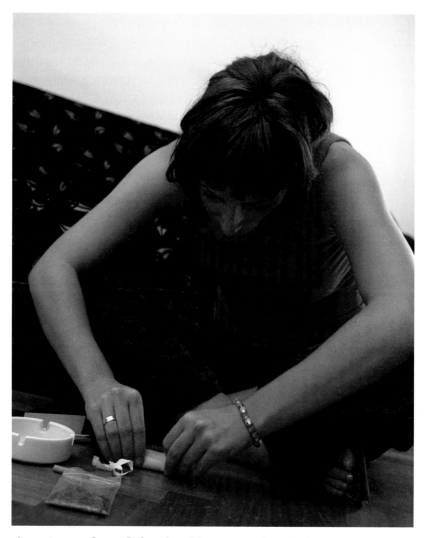

A major study at Columbia University found that residents of states with legal medical marijuana had marijuana abuse/ dependence rates almost twice as high as did states without such laws.

study published in *Drug and Alcohol Dependence* by researchers at Columbia University looked at two separate datasets and found that residents of states with medical marijuana had marijuana abuse/dependence rates almost twice as high than [had] states without such laws.

Most importantly, the studies discussed by NORML miss the mark, by failing to take into account the actual implementation of medical marijuana laws. For example, California did not have "dispensaries" until 2003, seven years after the law was enacted. And Rhode Island, the state used in the Brown study, had about 1,500 people in the entire program, so it's not a revelation that the state would not see any significant effect on teens. Time will tell, with further study and analysis, how medical marijuana is affecting attitudes and use rates in the long term.

What of course is never talked about is how medical marijuana programs in states that have gone full steam ahead actually work. Rarely mentioned is the fact that, for example, according to a 2011 study in the *Journal of Drug Policy Analysis* that examined 1,655 applicants in California who sought a physician's recommendation for medical marijuana, very few of those who sought a recommendation had cancer, HIV/AIDS, glaucoma, or multiple sclerosis. A study published in the *Harm Reduction Journal* (not exactly an anti-drug mouthpiece), analyzing over 3,000 "medical marijuana" users in California, found that an overwhelming majority (87.9%) of those queried about the details of their marijuana initiation had tried it before the age of 19, and the average user was a 32-year-old white male. 74% of the Caucasians in the sample had used cocaine, and over 50% had used methamphetamine in their lifetime. Hardly any had life-threatening illnesses.

Changing Attitudes Towards Marijuana Make Teen Use More Likely

Finally, we know from other surveys like the University of Michigan *Monitoring the Future* study that the perceived harm for smoking marijuana occasionally or regularly has been decreasing among the 8th grade since 2007. Social disapproval for smoking marijuana once or twice, occasionally, and regularly has been decreasing among 8th graders since 2007. That has translated into a major increase in use, which is no surprise to researchers who know that attitudes affect youth use rates.

Marijuana Perceived Risk Versus Past-Year Use by Twelfth Graders

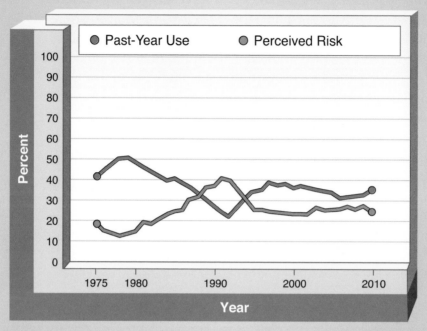

Based on data from University of Michigan, 2011 Monitoring the Future Study.

Taken from: NIDA [National Institute on Drug Abuse]. "DrugFacts: High School and Youth Trends," revised July 2012.
http://m.drugabuse.gov.

And how can we say that today's medical marijuana programs aren't having an effect on youth attitudes toward the drug? "Marijuana is medicine" has become a common slogan in America today, as people like Dr. Christian Thurstone, a Colorado doctor working with kids, [on February 10, 2010,] talked about on National Public Radio.

It's time to get the legalization lobby out of the business of medical marijuana and instead focus our attention on scientists developing non-smoked marijuana-based medications for the truly ill. That would make this issue no longer the sick joke that it is today.

SIX

Medical Marijuana Does Not Significantly Increase Recreational Use by Teenagers

William Breathes

William Breathes is the pen name of a graduate student, journalist, and medical marijuana patient in Denver, Colorado. In the following viewpoint Breathes refutes claims that medical marijuana is responsible for increased recreational use of the drug by teenagers. He says that while it is true that medical and recreational use of marijuana is becoming more acceptable in society, young people are also continuously exposed to advertising telling them that tobacco and alcohol, both of which are very harmful drugs, are socially acceptable. According to Breathes, young people are probably getting *some* medical marijuana via dishonest people who break the law in providing it to them, but the medical dispensaries themselves are not to blame because they do not sell marijuana to minors. He notes that young people have been able to get their hands on marijuana for many decades before medical marijuana became available, and points out that young people also manage to get alcohol illegally using fake identification or asking adults to get it for them.

Over the last four years [2008–2012], drug violations at Colorado K–12 [kindergarten through grade twelve] schools have increased by roughly 45 percent.

And according to a report shared by Education News Colorado about the issue, the rise can be squarely attributed to medical marijuana dispensaries.

Though the data doesn't distinguish between marijuana and other drugs, including pharmaceuticals, the report cites "school and district officials, healthcare workers and students" as saying marijuana is the reason behind the spike.

They believe there is a shift in perception about cannabis use among students. The report alleges that because medical marijuana shops are so abundant in Colorado, the message being sent to kids is that marijuana is harmless.

Shifting Attitudes

"When I grew up, it was horrible if you got caught with pot," says East [(Denver) High School] teacher Matt Murphy in the report. "Now there are little green medical signs everywhere. It seems healthy. We're at the front lines of this huge shift where kids think it's okay."

Oh, the horror. Maybe that's because to 32 percent of the nation, medical marijuana *is* okay and perfectly legal. Attitudes are also shifting toward recreational use, with nearly half the country in favor of legalization for adult use, according to some polls. Meanwhile, kids are exposed day in and day out to liquor ads and tobacco ads on television and in print telling them in more ways than one that these deadly products are acceptable.

Among some of the other points raised:

- Overall, suspensions were down 11 percent and expulsions were down 25 percent in infractions not involving drugs.
- Denver saw a 71 percent increase in drug violations referred to law enforcement. East High School violations have tripled since 2009.
- In 2010, Denver police started noting marijuana arrests separately from other drugs. That school year, the DPD [Denver

Police Department] made 179 arrests at 43 different elementary, middle and high schools.

- Schools with the largest increase in drug violations have "multiple medical marijuana dispensaries" within a mile.
- The report also includes a map of all schools and dispensaries around the state.

Medical Marijuana Dispensaries Are Not to Blame

Of course, all of this misses a big point: Kids have been getting their hands on marijuana and smoking it for the last forty years or more with or without dispensaries around. I speak from experience growing up in a medical marijuana–less state.

California Youths' Marijuana Use (from 1996 to 2008)

In 1996 California passed Proposition 215, legalizing medical marijuana under state law. Twelve years later, levels of recreational use had dropped among teenagers in grades 7, 9, and 11.

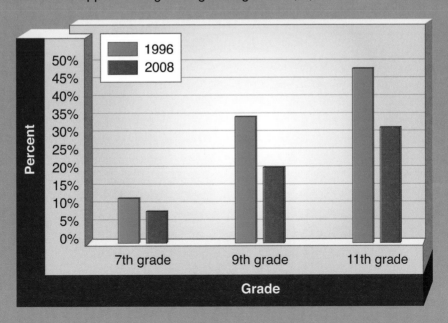

Taken from: Karen O'Keefe. "Marijuana Use by Young People: The Impact of State Medical Marijuana Laws [updated: June 2011]". Marijuana Policy Project, June 2011. www.mpp.org.

Now, I'm not stupid enough to say that the increased availability of herb hasn't contributed somewhat to the rise. But the blame shouldn't be cast on dispensaries that have never sold to illegal minors. Rather, it belongs on dishonest people abusing the system. And that's not germane to just medical marijuana dispensaries; neither is it a recent phenomenon.

The report uses the term "shoulder tapping" to refer to underage kids standing outside a dispensary asking people to buy them weed, as if that's a new issue. It's not. Kids have been doing that for booze for much, much longer—and are going to continue doing it.

According to a report shared by Education News Colorado, the rise in teenage marijuana use in Colorado is directly attributable to the many marijuana dispensaries in operation in that state.

And that's not including the thousands of purchases made by kids using fake IDs or with the assistance of careless liquor store owners or bartenders. In Boulder during 2010 alone, police used underage decoys showing their real IDs in 469 liquor-store stings, busting more than 59 stores that sold to the minors. You want to talk about a problem? Booze kills more teens each year in Colorado than cannabis has ever killed in the thousands of years humans have been using it. But do we blame the entire liquor industry for this? Hardly.

Meanwhile, as attorney Brian Vicente points out in the report, not a single illegal underage transaction has ever been reported from dispensaries—which require a medical marijuana card to even get through the secured entrance most all shops have.

Vicente's conclusion? Students are getting marijuana the same way they have been for years: illegally.

SEVEN

Medical Marijuana Research Is Blocked by Federal Agencies

Marijuana Policy Project

The Marijuana Policy Project (MPP) is the largest marijuana policy reform organization in the United States, working to remove criminal penalties for marijuana use and to make marijuana medically available to seriously ill people who have the approval of their doctors. In the following viewpoint, which is a memo from the MPP's website, the authors argue that medical marijuana research is consistently blocked by federal agencies, especially the National Institute on Drug Abuse (NIDA). NIDA has a monopoly on supplying marijuana for research and, according to the authors, is biased against research that attempts to show marijuana's medicinal value. For example, when Dr. Donald Abrams wanted to study marijuana's potential in treating HIV/AIDS wasting syndrome, NIDA refused, instead requesting that he study the *risks* in using marijuana to treat such patients and required that he not use patients suffering from the wasting syndrome in the study. The authors say NIDA also takes too long to respond to research requests (two years in one case) and that the marijuana they have is not very well suited for the research studies that need to be done.

Although 17 states and the District of Columbia have approved medical marijuana laws [as of September 2012], the Institute of Medicine's call for expanded clinical trials on marijuana's medical safety and efficacy remains largely unfulfilled. In 2008, the American College of Physicians noted that "research expansion has been hindered by a complicated federal approval process [and] limited availability of research-grade marijuana. . . ." In addition to the standard FDA [Food and Drug Administration] and DEA [Drug Enforcement Administration] approvals needed for all research using Schedule I drugs [drugs deemed under the Controlled Substances Act to have a high potential for abuse and no medical usefulness], researchers conducting trials with marijuana must receive approval through a National Institute on Drug Abuse/Public Health Service (NIDA/PHS) protocol review process that exists for *no other drug*.

Over a dozen recent small-scale Phase 2[1] clinical trials have found support for marijuana's medical efficacy. However, NIDA's monopoly on the federally approved marijuana supply, federal obstruction of privately-funded research, and a lack of public funding for research have created a catch-22: While more than a million Americans find relief under state medical marijuana laws, they often hear that there is not enough large-scale Phase 3 research to make marijuana available by prescription. Yet, the deck is stacked against that research happening.

NIDA's Institutional Bias Results in Delays and Refusals for Research

NIDA has a monopoly on the supply of marijuana that can be legally used in federally approved research—unlike other Schedule 1 drugs. NIDA also has a bias against research intended to evaluate marijuana's medical efficacy. NIDA's Stephen Gust testified "that it is not NIDA's mission to study medicinal uses of marijuana. . . ." Rather, the federal agency that has sole responsibility for

---

1. Phase 1 trials determine basic safety; phase 2 trials determine the clinical effectiveness of a medication and further test safety; phase 3 trials are large-scale studies to provide a final determination of the safety and effectiveness of a proposed medication.

"Medical Marijuana Smoking Accessories," cartoon by Steve Greenberg. Reproduced by permission. steve@greenberg-art.com

supplying (or not supplying) marijuana for research is charged with "support[ing] research on the causes, consequences, prevention, and treatment of drug abuse and drug addiction."

As the DEA's chief administrative law judge found, "NIDA's system for evaluating requests for marijuana research has resulted in some researchers who hold DEA registrations and the requisite approval from the Department of Health and Human Services being unable to conduct their research because NIDA has refused to provide them with marijuana." In 1995, Dr. Donald Abrams developed a research protocol to study marijuana's potential benefits for HIV/AIDS wasting syndrome patients. Dr. Abrams received the requisite approvals, but NIDA denied his application to obtain marijuana after first refusing to respond for nine months. After Proposition 215 [legalizing medical marijuana under state law] passed in California in 1996, NIDA asked Dr. Abrams to study the *risks* of marijuana use in HIV/AIDS patients, but NIDA insisted that subjects with AIDS wasting syndrome be excluded from the study. When Dr. Abrams accepted, NIDA not only provided the marijuana, it paid one million dollars for the study. In

1999, NIDA refused to supply marijuana to Dr. Ethan Russo for a marijuana/migraine study that had been approved by the FDA.

In addition, the NIDA/PHS review has no deadlines and no formal appeals process, in contrast to the FDA's 30-day deadline. The Institute of Medicine recommended the development of a smoke-free delivery system, yet NIDA has obstructed research on such a device. NIDA took more than two years before it rejected a protocol requesting to buy 10 grams of marijuana to study a smokeless vaporizer, without human subjects. MAPS [Multidisciplinary Association for Psychedelic Studies] director Rick Doblin testified that developing marijuana into a prescription medicine "is MAPS' explicit goal, so . . . anything we do gets shut down." In 2011, NIDA refused to supply MAPS with marijuana for an FDA-approved PTSD [post-traumatic stress disorder] study. MAPS can apply again, but approval requires unanimous consent from a committee that gave contradictory guidance.

NIDA's Monopoly Is a Barrier to Private Research

In addition to failing to provide marijuana to FDA-approved protocols, NIDA's monopoly deters potential privately-funded researchers because financial sponsors will not invest millions of dollars in clinical research until there is reliable access to a supply of marijuana that can be used both in research and—if it resulted in FDA approval—as a prescription medicine. NIDA is not authorized by Congress to sell marijuana for prescription use, yet the same strain would have to be used in research and as the approved drug. Another barrier is that pharmaceutical companies have a financial incentive to research isolated compounds of marijuana—which they can patent—rather than the whole plant, which they cannot.

NIDA's marijuana has often been freeze-dried for years. It has low concentrations of THC [tetrahydrocannabinol, the main active ingredient of marijuana] and includes virtually no cannabidiol, which has therapeutic value. Other producers could produce marijuana with a better safety profile.

Since 2001, Professor Lyle Craker, Ph.D., University of Massachusetts–Amherst Medicinal Plant Program, has unsuccessfully attempted to acquire a license from the DEA to grow marijuana for research. On February 12, 2007, DEA Administrative Law Judge Mary Ellen Bittner recommended granting Dr. Craker a license, finding that it would be in the public interest for the DEA to issue Dr. Craker a license, and that the DEA's refusal to grant additional licenses to grow marijuana resulted in inadequate competition and a current supply that was inadequate for research needs. However, the DEA delayed responding to Judge Bittner's recommendation for almost two years, then rejected her recommendation on January 14, 2009, six days before the inauguration of President [Barack] Obama.

The Federal Government Is Not Sufficiently Funding Research

Despite the fact that more than 30% of Americans live in jurisdictions that allow the medical use of marijuana, the federal government has provided almost no funding for clinical studies on marijuana's efficacy since those state laws passed. The federal government provided marijuana for free to more than a dozen patients for many years in its Investigational New Drug Program, but has failed to conduct any research on marijuana's efficacy in treating their conditions. Four patients in the program, who have received marijuana for 19 or more years, survive today. The only study of these patients was privately funded. It found, "Cannabis smoking, even of a crude, low-grade product, provides effective symptomatic relief of pain, muscle spasms, and intraocular [inside the eye] pressure elevations. . . ."

The California Legislature funded and created the Center for Medicinal Cannabis Research (CMCR) to study marijuana's medical efficacy. In February 2010, the CMCR released a report on its 15 completed or ongoing studies, finding support for marijuana's efficacy at alleviating pain and reducing spasms. However, no further funding has been allocated, and, in this time of economic downturn, no other states are known to be funding

The Marijuana Policy Project (MPP) delivers boxes containing 252,000 signatures supporting medical marijuana legalization in Arizona. MPP is the largest marijuana policy reform organization in the United States.

similar studies. Due to the factors outlined in this memo, experts are aware of very few current clinical studies on the medical efficacy of smoked or vaporized whole plant marijuana in the U.S.—only the ongoing CMCR studies and one additional study. Non-profit organizations with private funding are ready and eager to fund full-scale FDA-approved drug development research into a range of potential medical uses of marijuana once the DEA is forced to end the NIDA monopoly on the supply of marijuana for research. Even then, the process to make marijuana available by prescription is expected to take about 10 years, so state laws are needed to protect patients in the meantime.

EIGHT

Editorial: Welcome Start Toward Humane Policing of Pot

Orange County Register

The following selection is a staff editorial from the *Orange County Register*, a Pulitzer Prize–winning newspaper based in Santa Ana, California, and founded in 1905. In the following viewpoint the authors argue that marijuana is improperly classified under the Controlled Substances Act, a federal law passed in 1970 that places drugs into five different "schedules," or categories. Currently marijuana is placed in Schedule 1, the most restricted category, meaning it has no currently accepted medical use, cannot be used safely (even under medical supervision), and has a high potential for abuse. According to the authors, marijuana does not fit any of the requirements of Schedule 1—in particular, an increasing amount of scientific evidence shows that it helps alleviate certain medical conditions. If marijuana is placed in a less restrictive schedule, doctors would be allowed to prescribe it, a step the authors say is necessary to prevent the federal government from interfering in states that have legalized medical marijuana.

It took the Obama administration some time—after declaring that federal officials would not go after patients and providers in states with valid medical marijuana laws—to issue an official memorandum to that effect, and the memorandum contains loopholes a rogue prosecutor could exploit. But the memorandum for selected United States attorneys is nonetheless welcome, and a huge step in the direction of common-sense, humane enforcement policies.

The next logical step is to eliminate marijuana or cannabis from the list, or schedule, of drugs no doctor can legally prescribe—a step arguably called for by the Controlled Substances Act itself—and allow doctors nationwide to prescribe cannabis for patients who can benefit from it.

President Barack Obama, speaking here at the Interior Department, says he will not seek legal action against the states of Washington and Colorado for legalizing marijuana for all use.

Before we pick nits, it is appropriate to celebrate. Despite 13 states, including California, having passed laws permitting physicians to recommend marijuana to patients, and despite a growing body of scientific evidence documenting the efficacy of marijuana at alleviating certain medical conditions, the Drug Enforcement Administration has conducted occasional raids on cannabis patients and medical cannabis distribution facilities in California and other states.

Percentage of Patients Who Use Medical Marijuana as a Prescription Drug Substitute

In an anonymous survey of 350 patients at Berkeley Patients Group, a medical marijuana dispensary in Berkeley, California, 66% of patients indicated that they used marijuana instead of prescription drugs because it has fewer side effects and offers better symptom control. The director of the clinic, Amanda Reiman explains that "instead of having pain medication, an antianxiety medication, and a sleep medication, [patients] are able to just use cannabis, and that controls all of those symptoms."

34%
do not use marijuana
as a substitute for
perscription drugs

66%
use marijuana as a
perscription drug substitute

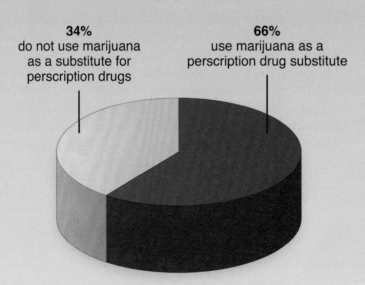

Taken from: Alexander M. Otto. "Medical Marijuana Often Used as a Prescription Drug Substitute." *Clinical Psychiatry News*, January, 2012.

These activities have encouraged a few local officials, who have never quite accepted this law, to harass patients, and has discouraged intelligent implementation of state laws. For the Justice Department to notify its prosecutors in states with medical cannabis laws that prosecution of patients and providers "is unlikely to be an efficient use of limited federal resources" is a very significant step.

It is unclear how significant it is, however, that the memorandum issued Monday is directed toward U.S. attorneys and not toward the Drug Enforcement Administration. It is obvious that some DEA agents still believe harassing cannabis patients is a worthwhile activity. Even if these cases are not prosecuted, as most of them are not, they are extremely disruptive of efforts to establish a legitimate "white market" for medical cannabis patients that would undermine the black market for recreational cannabis.

The memorandum also emphasizes that enforcing the general laws against marijuana possession and use is still a top priority. It spends more verbiage outlining circumstances in which prosecution might still be warranted than in explaining why it is unwise.

It seems clear, then, that "rescheduling" marijuana under the federal Controlled Substances Act is the next necessary step. Marijuana is now placed on Schedule I under the Act, which imposes complete prohibition and by law should be reserved only for substances with no known medical efficacy and a high propensity for abuse. The DOJ memorandum acknowledges what anybody who has investigated the matter knows: that marijuana does have legitimate medical uses, meaning it should not be on Schedule I. In fact, marijuana does not fit any of the criteria set out for being placed on Schedule I.

This step on prosecution is welcome, but it is only a first step toward a more sensible and humane policy. Rescheduling—a step well short of full legalization, which should also be open for discussion—is the next logical step.

NINE

Marijuana Should Not Be Federally Reclassified for Medical Use

Kevin A. Sabet

Kevin A. Sabet is a fellow at the Center for Substance Abuse Solutions at the University of Pennsylvania and served as senior adviser at the White House Office of National Drug Control Policy (ONDCP) from 2009 to 2011. In the following viewpoint Sabet argues that changing the legal classification of marijuana is unnecessary and will not solve problems with existing medical marijuana programs. Currently, under the Controlled Substances Act (CSA), marijuana is placed in Schedule 1, meaning it has no accepted medical use, cannot be used safely (even under medical supervision), and has a high potential for abuse. Some have suggested that conflicts between states with medical marijuana and the federal government, which considers any use of marijuana to be illegal, would be resolved by placing marijuana into a less restricted schedule under the CSA. Sabet disagrees, saying that any medication would still need to be approved as a medicine by the Food and Drug Administration (FDA) to be legally prescribed, and the FDA has explicitly rejected raw marijuana as a medicine. The author adds that some isolated components of marijuana have been approved as legal medicines, making smokable marijuana unnecessary for medical use.

On Wednesday [November 30, 2011], the governors of Washington and Rhode Island convened a press conference calling on the federal government to reclassify marijuana so as to acknowledge its medical value and allow its use, in their words, "for treatment—prescribed by doctors and filled by pharmacists."

Houston, we have a problem. Call it bad staff work or just an easy way for Governors Lincoln Chafee (D-RI) and Chris Gregoire (I-WA) to pass the buck to the Feds and dodge a highly volatile issue, but federal rescheduling will not do any of the things they are calling for. A few facts to consider: First, rescheduling marijuana would not allow doctors to prescribe the drug, nor would it make it okay for pharmacists to dispense the drug. The Food and Drug Administration (FDA) requires drugs to go through a rigorous safety and efficacy approval process before allowing any prescriptions to be written. Second—and this is a big one—marijuana-derived medications have *already* been rescheduled. Finally, it's worth noting that medical associations around the world agree that any medicine should be determined in the lab by the scientific process, not the ballot box.

Raw Marijuana Versus Isolated Components

Medical marijuana is a sticky subject, to be sure. No one wants to see their loved ones suffer needlessly, and there is a good case to be made that federal law enforcement should focus its limited resources on major drug producers and distributors.

But as recently as this past summer [2011], the FDA ruled that raw marijuana—which contains hundreds of unknown components—did not meet its general standards of safety and efficacy. And the drug failed an exhaustive eight-factor scientific analysis that examined hundreds of studies on the plant's health effects. The FDA's position has also been affirmed by independent scientific bodies like the National Academies of Sciences' Institute of Medicine (IOM), which famously determined that "there is little future in smoked marijuana as a medically approved medication."

This does not mean that marijuana has no medicinal value. Indeed, the FDA has determined that some elements found in marijuana are helpful to seriously ill patients, and the IOM also concluded that "if there is any future for marijuana as a medicine, it lies in its isolated components. . . ." Some of those components—like Marinol and Cesamet—are available to be prescribed today (though they aren't as popular as you might think—doctors generally find non-marijuana medications more effective for many conditions). But we don't smoke opium to reap the benefits of morphine, nor do we chew willow bark to receive the effects of aspirin. Similarly, we should not have to smoke marijuana to get potential therapeutic effects from its components.

Rescheduling Marijuana Will Not Solve Anything

Does that mean that our work investigating marijuana's components as a medicine is done? Of course not. Researchers are investigating other safe delivery methods for these types of medications, as well as the possible medical value of other elements within marijuana that we are just learning about. The National Institutes of Health funds a number of these studies. Research into how components of marijuana may affect our brains and bodies is an exciting area of science. Does marijuana's status as a Schedule I drug stop this research from happening? No. Could the Feds speed up the approval process for safe, marijuana-based medications and ensure that our scientific resources are adequately allocated? Of course, and I hope they will. Many of us who follow this area of science are excited about these drugs coming down the FDA pipeline. One such product is called Sativex, a mouth-spray containing two active components of the marijuana plant and already approved in several countries around the world.

But smoked marijuana is not medicine, and it is not based on science. Anyone living with smoked medical marijuana in their state knows that it has turned into a sad joke. A recent study found that the average "patient" was a 32-year-old white male with a history of drug and alcohol abuse and no history of a life-

Dronabinol, a Synthetic Cannabinoid, Reduces Pain and Increases Appetite in Clinical Trials

Studies of dronabinol (a synthetic form of THC, the main active ingredient in marijuana) found that it significantly reduced pain in MS (multiple sclerosis) patients, and increased appetite in AIDS (acquired immune deficiency syndrome) patients, compared to a placebo (a substance with no therapeutic effect).

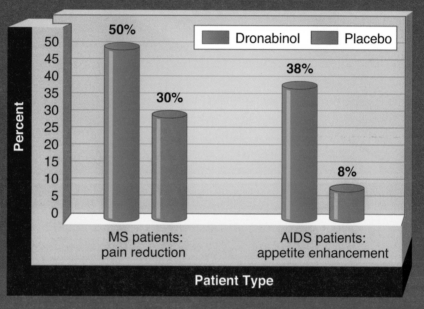

Taken from: Igor Grant et al. "Medical Marijuana: Clearing Away the Smoke." *Open Neurology Journal*, May 4, 2012. http://benthamscience.com.

threatening disease. Further studies have shown that very few of those who sought a recommendation for the drug had cancer, HIV/AIDS, glaucoma, or multiple sclerosis. We are also beginning to see a link between medical marijuana and increased drug use, according to a few recent, exhaustive studies.

So what explains this rather bizarre (and factually inaccurate) appeal by these two otherwise sensible governors? Politics. These officials, and many others, find themselves in a difficult spot—caught between laws that were intended to allow the limited use

The Controlled Substances Act classifies marijuana as a Schedule 1 drug, indicating that it has no medicinal value. Opponents of legalized medical marijuana think it should stay that way.

of marijuana for (ostensible) medical purposes and the reality of what that means when these laws are actually implemented—the headache of "dispensaries," increased drug use that results from rampant distribution of the drug, and a federal government determined to uphold existing law. It's not an envious position to be in, but it would make a whole lot of sense if these governors were taking their cues from the science and advocating for, say, expedited approval of a marijuana-derived drug like Sativex, which is not smoked and has a standard dose. Advocating for a policy that is impossible to implement and, more importantly, does not solve their conundrum in the first place diverts away from the real, complicated issues at hand. And it helps no one in the end.

TEN

Another Dance Around Marijuana

The Oregonian Editorial Board

In the following viewpoint, which was written by the editorial staff of *The Oregonian*, a daily newspaper based in Portland, Oregon, the authors argue that the medical marijuana movement is a covert attempt to legalize recreational marijuana. They discuss Initiative 28, a political initiative put before Oregon voters in 2010 that proposed to license farmers to grow marijuana for sale in medical dispensaries in that state. (The initiative did not pass.) According to the authors, such efforts are not really about medical marijuana but are actually intended to provide a legal form of recreational marijuana. They say that most of the 36,380 people in Oregon (as of July 2010) authorized to use medical marijuana did not have serious illnesses but were allegedly using it for "severe pain." The authors suggest that medical marijuana advocates be more honest about their true motivations instead of pretending that the issue is about providing medical marijuana to patients in need.

L et the charades begin: Another "medical marijuana" measure is coming to the fall ballot.

Of course, the advocates insist that the sprawling legalized network of marijuana dispensaries envisioned by Initiative 28 is all about providing compassionate and convenient "medicine" to Oregonians who suffer from such things as glaucoma, nausea from cancer treatment and the wasting associated with HIV/AIDs.

Never mind that of the 36,380 Oregon "patients" who now hold cards that protect them from state prosecution for smoking marijuana, 534 reported suffering from glaucoma, while 32,614 checked the box for "severe pain" as one of their qualifying medical conditions. Anyone over the age of 18 with a doctor's note that says they can benefit from smoking marijuana can apply to the Oregon Health Division for a card.

We're not yet prepared to take a position on this or any other ballot measure on the fall ballot. Yes, there may be a compelling case to be made for giving Oregonians with legitimate medical needs more convenient access to marijuana. However, the whole wink-and-nod farce that has characterized the politics of medical marijuana has become downright offensive.

Frankly, we'd much rather have the kind of open, intellectually honest debate they're having now down in Oakland, Calif., where the City Council just voted 5–2 to license four huge marijuana farms of up to 100,000 square feet apiece, and plan to use the tax revenue to close a $83 million city deficit this year. At least Californians, who have already had the pleasant high of seeing marijuana dispensaries crowd into mini-malls and storefronts in communities all across their states, are having an honest-to-goodness vote in November on legalizing recreational use of marijuana.

After all, that's what this is about. Forget the euphemisms—what after all, is a "dispensary" anyway? It's a store the state legally entitles to sell pot. What's going on here is nothing more or less than a backdoor effort to expand marijuana use while dancing gingerly around federal law that still prohibits the production, distribution and use of the drug.

"Mother, are you sure your marijuana use is purely medicinal?"

"Mother, Are You Sure Your Marijuana Use Is Purely Medicinal?" cartoon by Royston Robertson. www.CartoonStock.com.

Why not call the real question? Maybe a majority of Oregonians believe marijuana ought to be the legal and social equivalent of alcohol—produced and sold openly, regulated and taxed. Jeffrey Miron, a Harvard economist, has estimated that marijuana prohibition costs the nation $7 billion in tax revenue, not to mention the costs of the futile effort to police it. Maybe Oregonians want a piece of that for their underfunded schools and state government.

But then why continue the medical marijuana charade? Why all these "dispensaries" and this facade of regulation, such as the prohibition of anyone convicted of a felony crime in the past five

A medical marijuana grow site in Oregon. Many believe that the push to legalize medical marijuana is just a ploy to legalize marijuana for all uses, including recreational.

years from getting a license to open his or her marijuana store? Does that mean someone just finishing up a hitch of six years or more in Oregon State Prison for assault or rape would be a fine proprietor of your neighborhood marijuana dispensary? Who knows? Who cares?

Not supporters of Initiative 28. Ultimately, their measure isn't about medical marijuana or people suffering with glaucoma or nausea. It's about moving ever closer to a future of legalized recreational use of marijuana. If they are so certain that would be good for Oregonians, they ought to have the courage to call the question.

ELEVEN

To End the Ambiguity of Medical Marijuana, Marijuana Should Be Fully Legalized

Nolan Finley

Nolan Finley is the editorial page editor of *The Detroit News*. In the following viewpoint Finley argues that legalizing medical marijuana in Michigan and other states has created an ambiguous situation in which there is no clear line between medical and recreational use. In the state of Michigan, where he lives, there is no distinction between the way marijuana is produced and marketed for medical or recreational use, leaving authorities confused as to what is legal and what is not—medical marijuana clinics are allowed to operate freely in some places and are shut down by authorities in other areas. According to the author, medical marijuana is, as critics claim, a step toward full legalization of the drug, and he suggests that legalization is the best course of action because it would end the confusion surrounding medical marijuana, bring in much-needed tax revenue, and save money currently used to enforce laws against recreational use.

This was as predictable as the sunrise—Michigan voters overwhelmingly passed a ballot measure to legalize medical marijuana [in 2008], and two years later, no one can seem to decide who's a patient and who's a pothead.

More than 60,000 residents have applied for medical marijuana certificates, the ticket to being able to use pot legally, and even grow small amounts at home; roughly half have received them. Wow, that's a lot of suffering in our state.

Perhaps when voters passed the proposal in 2008 they envisioned cancer and glaucoma patients toking in the restricted confines of hospitals and clinics, and getting sanitized pot in carefully measured doses from licensed pharmacies.

An Ambiguous Situation

That's not exactly how it's worked out. Therapeutic pot is being marketed about the same way as the everyday let's-get-high-for-the-hell-of-it pot. It's being grown in basements under hot lights and pushed to patients through head shops and person-to-person deals that have the law enforcement community struggling to figure out what's legal and what isn't.

The answer seems to depend on where you live. Oakland County, for example, is busy putting the pot stores out of business and cracking down on the home growers; Ann Arbor has 23 medical marijuana stores that go unmolested by authorities.

And it's not just cops and judges who are confused. Employers have fired medical marijuana patients for failing drug tests, even though the law prohibits that, and landlords have evicted users for violating no-dope clauses in their leases.

You don't have to be struggling with the effects of chemotherapy to qualify for a certificate. The medical marijuana industry has physicians lined up to certify patients with mysterious pains, anxiety and other ailments often visible only to the sufferer. The law isn't very specific on the diseases covered. Chronic headaches can get you approved, and who doesn't have headaches these days?

Support for Making Use of Marijuana Legal

The Gallup polling agency has been asking Americans how they feel about legalizing marijuana since 1969. Over time, the percentage supporting marijuana legalization has gradually increased. As of 2011, more people favored legalization than opposed it.

Do you think the use of marijuana should be made legal or not?

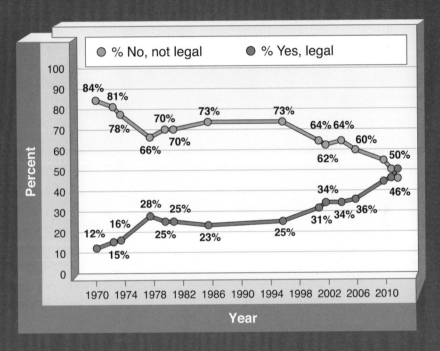

Taken from: Gallup. "Record-High 50% of Americans Favor Legalizing Marijuana Use," October 17, 2011. www.gallup.com.

Full Legalization Is the Solution

Kids roam downtown events passing out cards with 800-numbers and websites where you can get certificates. This isn't what voters envisioned, but it's what they've got now, and putting the genie back in the bong is impossible.

A man walks into a Michigan medical marijuana dispensary. Critics argue that Michigan's medical marijuana law is ambiguous and there is no clear line between medical and recreational use.

Critics of medical marijuana have called it the first step toward legalizing all pot use. They're right. And it should be.

It's absurd for Michigan to still be arresting and jailing pot growers and users whose only real crime is that they were too stupid to apply for a medical marijuana certificate.

Give it up. Stop wasting taxpayer money in a futile fight to keep marijuana away from the people who want to use it. If current trends continue, most pot users will soon have a license to smoke anyway.

Better to focus our efforts on bringing the marijuana growers out of their basements and onto the tax rolls. Michigan could use the estimated $32 million in annual tax revenue it would generate, and the untold savings in law enforcement and corrections costs.

What You Should Know About Medical Marijuana

The Impact of Medical Marijuana Laws on Marijuana Use by Teens

According to a 2011 study by Melanie Wall et al., published in the *Annals of Epidemiology*:

- States that had legalized medical marijuana had an 8.68 percent rate of marijuana use by teenagers between 2002 and 2008.
- States without legalized medical marijuana had a rate of use among teenagers of 6.94 percent.
- Of eight states that have passed legislation legalizing medical marijuana since 2004, higher levels of teenage marijuana use and lower perception of risk existed prior to legalization compared to states that have not legalized medical marijuana.

According to the June 2011 report *Marijuana Use by Young People: The Impact of State Medical Marijuana Laws*, published by the Marijuana Policy Project:

- California, which legalized medical marijuana in 1996, has seen an overall decline in recreational marijuana use by teenagers.
- Washington, which legalized medical marijuana in 1998, has seen significant declines in use by teens.
- Oregon, which also legalized marijuana for medical use in 1998, has seen a moderate decline in current and lifetime use by teens.

- Maine, which legalized medical marijuana in 1999, has shown rates of use remaining constant or decreasing for all age groups since that time, and significant declines of current and lifetime use for high school students.
- Rhode Island, which legalized medical marijuana in 2006, has seen a small decline in lifetime use by teens, along with a slight increase in current use.
- Michigan, which legalized medical marijuana in 2008, has shown increases in current and lifetime use for students in grades eleven and twelve but declines in current and lifetime rates for students in grades nine and ten.
- Nationally, data from the Youth Risk Behavior Surveillance System (YRBSS) indicates that past-month recreational use of marijuana among high school students was 25.3 percent in 1995 (before the first state medical marijuana law was passed), declining to 20.8 percent in 2009.
- Lifetime use (i.e., has ever used marijuana) among high school students declined from 42.4 percent in 1995 to 36.8 percent in 2009.

The preliminary discussion paper "Medical Marijuana Laws and Teen Marijuana Use" by Mark Anderson et al., published in May 2012, reported the following:

- Between 1993 and 2009, when thirteen states legalized medical marijuana, the probability of youth having smoked marijuana in the previous thirty days in those states increased by no more than 1.4 percent.
- The probability of youth smoking marijuana frequently increased by no more than 0.4 percent.
- This is much less than the increase of 4.3 percent in past-month use nationwide among students in grade twelve between 2006 and 2011.

According to a report by Stacy Salomonsen-Sautel et al., published in the *Journal of the American Academy of Child & Adolescent Psychiatry* in July 2012:

- 73.8 percent of teenagers in treatment for substance abuse in Denver, Colorado, reported having used diverted medical marijuana (i.e., recommended by a doctor for someone else);
- teens reported having done so between one and a thousand times, with a median of fifty times;
- of the 164 patients studied, only 4 had applied for a medical marijuana card of their own, and only 1 of those had received a card.

The Economic Impact of Medical Marijuana

According to See Change Strategy's report *The State of the Medical Marijuana Markets 2011*:

- In 2011 the US national market in medical marijuana was valued at $1.7 billion.
- By 2016 it could be worth as much as $8.9 billion.
- Of all medical marijuana sales in 2011, 92 percent were accounted for by only two states: Colorado and California.
- The California market in medical marijuana was $1.3 billion in 2011.
- In 2011, 24.8 million people could qualify as medical marijuana patients according to existing state law.
- The estimated underground/illegal market in marijuana is $18 billion.
- Of wholesale and retail medical marijuana suppliers in 2011, 63 percent had been operating for less than one year.
- Thirty-four percent of wholesale/retail operators say that compliance with regulations, rather than demand or supply, is their greatest challenge.
- Twenty-four percent say that securing financing is their greatest challenge.

Characteristics of Medical Marijuana Users

According to the study "Who Are Medical Marijuana Patients? Population Characteristics from Nine California Assessment Clinics," published in the *Journal of Psychoactive Drugs* in 2011:

- 72.9 percent of medical marijuana (MM) patients in California were male, compared with 49.3 percent of the general population;
- 27.1 percent of MM patients were female, compared with 50.7 percent of the general population;
- 61.5 percent were white, compared with 59.5 percent of the general population;
- 14.4 percent were Latino, compared with 32.4 percent of the general population;
- 11.8 percent were African American, compared with 6.7 percent of the general population;
- 4.5 percent were Native American, compared with 1 percent of the general population;
- 17.9 percent were 18–24 years old, compared with 17.1 percent of the general population;
- 27.5 percent were 25–34, compared with 15.4 percent of the general population;
- 21.3 percent were 25–34, compared with 16.2 percent of the general population;
- 20.4 percent were 45–54, compared with 12.8 percent of the general population;
- 12.6 percent were 55 or older, compared with 18.4 percent of the general population;
- 64.8 percent of patients were employed;
- 73.4 percent had health insurance;
- 29.4 percent of MM patients reported using tobacco, compared with 25 percent of the general population;
- 47.5 percent of MM patients reported using alcohol, compared with 61.9 percent of the general population;
- 0.3 percent of MM patients reported using cocaine, compared with 1.9 percent of the general population;
- 50.9 percent said that MM was a substitute for prescription medication; and
- 13 percent said MM was a substitute for alcohol.
- Therapeutic benefits of medical marijuana reported by patients included:
  - pain relief (82.6 percent)
  - relief from muscle spasms (41.1 percent)

- headache relief (40.7 percent)
- relief of anxiety (37.8 percent)
- relief of nausea or vomiting (27.7 percent)
- relief from depression (26.1 percent)
- relief from cramps (19 percent)
- relief from panic attacks (16.9 percent)
- relief from diarrhea (5 percent)
- relief from itching (2.8 percent)
- improved sleep (70.7 percent)
- improved relaxation (55.1 percent)
- increased appetite (37.7 percent)
- increased concentration or focus (22.9 percent)
- increased energy (15.9 percent)
- prevention of side effects from medication (22.5 percent)
- prevention of anger (22.4 percent)
- prevention of involuntary movements (6.2 percent)
- prevention of seizures (3.2 percent)

- Physicians recommended MM for the following complaints:
  - back/spine/neck pain (30.6 percent)
  - sleep disorders (15.7 percent)
  - anxiety/depression (13 percent)
  - muscle spasms (9.5 percent)
  - arthritis (8.5 percent)
  - injuries to knee, ankle, foot (4.5 percent)
  - joint disease/disorders (4.4 percent)
  - narcolepsy (3.7 percent)
  - nausea (3.4 percent)
  - nerve/spine inflammation (2.9 percent)
  - headaches/migraines (2.7 percent)
  - eating disorders (1.1 percent)

Public Opinion on Medical Marijuana
According to a briefing paper released by the Marijuana Policy Project in 2011:

- Eighty-one percent of Americans polled by ABC News/ *Washington Post* on January 18, 2010, agreed that "doctors should be allowed to prescribe marijuana for medical purposes to treat their patients," a 12 percent increase from 1997.
- In 1990 a scientific survey of oncologists (doctors specializing in cancer treatment) revealed that:
  - 54 percent of those who had an opinion on the subject were in favor of marijuana being medically available; and
  - 44 percent had suggested at least once in their careers that a patient get marijuana illegally.

Gallup reported in October 2011 that:

- in 2010, 70 percent of Americans were in favor of allowing doctors to prescribe medical marijuana;
- 12 percent of Americans in 1969 were in favor of fully legalizing marijuana (i.e., for recreational as well as medical use), with 84 percent opposed;
- in 2000 support for full legalization passed 30 percent of the US population;
- in 2009 support passed 40 percent;
- as of October 2011 support for full legalization had reached 50 percent;
- 62% of eighteen- to twenty-nine-year-olds in 2011 favored legalizing marijuana, versus only 31 percent of those sixty-five and older.

A *Reason*-Rupe poll conducted in September 2012 reported that:

- 48 percent of respondents believed small amounts of marijuana for personal consumption should be legal for adults, while 48 percent did not believe marijuana should be legal for personal use;
- 59 percent of respondents under thirty-four are in favor of legalizing marijuana;
- 73 percent believed doctors should be allowed to prescribe medical marijuana, while 24 percent believed it should not be legal for doctors to prescribe marijuana.

What You Should Do About Medical Marijuana

Gather Information

The first step in grappling with any complex and controversial issue is to be informed about it. Gather as much information as you can from a variety of sources. The essays in this book form an excellent starting point, representing a variety of viewpoints and approaches to the topic. Your school or local library will be another source of useful information; look there for relevant books, magazines, and encyclopedia entries. The Bibliography and Organizations to Contact sections of this book will give you useful starting points in gathering additional information.

There is a wealth of data and perspectives on medical marijuana in both the US and international media. Internet search engines will be helpful to you in your research; note that *cannabis* is another commonly used term for marijuana and may yield additional search results. Many blogs and websites have information and articles dealing with the topic from a variety of viewpoints, including concerned individuals offering their opinions, activist organizations, governmental organizations such as the National Institute on Drug Abuse, and popular media outlets.

Many articles, books, and other resources dealing with this topic have been published in recent years. As well, an increasing number of academic papers on medical marijuana are available. If the information in such papers is too dense or technical, check the abstract at the beginning of the article, which provides a clear summary of the researcher's conclusions.

Identify the Issues

Once you have gathered your information, review it methodically to discover the key issues involved.

Why do some people use medical marijuana, as opposed to more conventional medication? How is medical marijuana produced and distributed? What are the differences between marijuana in its natural form and pharmaceutical medications based on extracts or synthetic versions of its active ingredients? In terms of risks and benefits, how does marijuana compare to other medications that are commonly used? As a recreational drug, how does it compare to other recreational drugs, such as alcohol and tobacco, which are in common use? How does medical marijuana legislation differ in the various states in which it has been legalized? What is the federal government's position on marijuana as medicine, and how does that affect the effort of states to legalize the practice in their own jurisdictions? How has the recreational use of marijuana or the prohibition of the drug affected its use as medicine, people's attitudes toward its medical use, or the medical marijuana movement itself? It may be worthwhile to consider how the use of marijuana as medicine has worked in other cultures and time periods, to get a broader perspective on what is happening in America today.

Evaluate Your Information Sources

In developing your own opinion, it is vital to evaluate the sources of the information you have discovered. Authors of books, magazine articles, etc., however well intentioned, have their own perspectives and biases that may affect how they present information on the subject. Medical marijuana is a controversial and complicated issue, particularly given its additional role as a popular but illegal recreational drug, and people regard it in very different ways. In some cases people and organizations may deliberately or unconsciously distort information to support a strongly held ideological or moral position—signs of this include oversimplification and extreme positions.

Consider the author's credentials and what organizations he or she is affiliated with. Attitudes toward medical marijuana vary depending on the beliefs of the people or agencies involved. For example, those who work with drug addicts, or agencies tasked with enforcing antidrug laws, may view marijuana as a harmful drug and oppose legalizing *any* use of the plant. Conversely, those who work in the medical marijuana industry will see it in a much more positive light and may downplay any harmful effects or unintended consequences of the medical marijuana movement or of marijuana itself. If, during your research, you find someone arguing against their expected bias—for example, a police officer arguing in favor of legalizing medical marijuana, or a medical marijuana advocate opposing a marijuana legalization initiative—it may be worthwhile to pay particular attention to what they are saying. Always critically evaluate and assess your sources rather than take whatever they say at face value.

Examine Your Own Perspective

Medical marijuana is a complex and emotionally charged topic. Spend some time exploring your own thoughts and feelings about it. Consider the attitudes and beliefs on this issue that you have received from family members, friends, and the media throughout your life. Such messages affect your own thoughts and feelings about the subject. Have you or anyone you know ever used marijuana in a medical or recreational context? If you or someone close to you has experienced significant difficulties or negative consequences as a result of drug use or addiction, that may make it more challenging to form a clear view of the issues surrounding medical marijuana, and/or it may give you special insight into the topic. Be wary of "confirmation bias," the tendency to seek out information that confirms what one already believes to be true and to discount information that contradicts preexisting beliefs. Deliberately counter this tendency by seeking out perspectives that contradict your current attitudes.

Form Your Own Opinion and Take Action

Once you have gathered and organized such information, identified the issues involved, and examined your own perspective, you will be ready to form an opinion on medical marijuana and to advocate your position in debates and discussions. You may even decide to take a more active role in the debate. Many organizations on all sides of the issue are working hard to effect change (or maintain the status quo) on medical and recreational use of marijuana—check out the Organizations to Contact section in this book for some starting points if you want to get more involved.

Perhaps you will conclude that one of the viewpoints you have encountered on medical marijuana offers the best approach to the issue, or you may decide that a number of approaches working together are needed to adequately address this complex topic. You might even decide that none of the perspectives that you have encountered are convincing to you and that you cannot yet take a decisive position. If that is the case, ask yourself what you would need to know to make up your mind; perhaps a bit more research would be helpful. Whatever position you take, be prepared to explain it clearly based on facts, evidence, and well-thought-out opinions.

The editors have compiled the following list of organizations concerned with the issues debated in this book. The descriptions are derived from materials provided by the organizations. All have publications or information available for interested readers. The list was compiled on the date of publication of the present volume; names, addresses, phone and fax numbers, and e-mail and Internet addresses may change. Be aware that many organizations take several weeks or longer to respond to inquiries, so allow as much time as possible.

American Civil Liberties Union (ACLU)
125 Broad St., 18th Fl., New York, NY 10004
(212) 549-2500
e-mail: aclu@aclu.org
website: www.aclu.org

The ACLU is a national organization that works to defend Americans' civil rights guaranteed by the US Constitution. It provides legal defense, research, and education. The ACLU opposes the criminalization of marijuana and the resulting civil liberties violations. Its publications include *ACLU Briefing Paper #19: Against Drug Prohibition* and *Ira Glasser on Marijuana Myths and Facts*. Searching for "medical marijuana" on its website yields well over a hundred hits. Of particular note is the website's page on marijuana law reform (www.aclu.org/criminal-law-reform /marijuana-law-reform).

Americans for Safe Access (ASA)
1600 Clay St., Ste. 600
Oakland, CA 94612
(510) 251-1856
fax: (510)251-2036

e-mail: info@safeaccessnow.org
website: http://safeaccessnow.org

ASA is a national grassroots coalition working with local, state, and national legislators to protect the rights of patients and doctors to legally use marijuana for medical purposes. It provides legal training for lawyers and patients, medical information for doctors and patients, media support for court cases, activist training for grassroots organizers, and rapid response to law enforcement encounters. ASA sends out e-mail alerts to update its members on legal cases and current events pertaining to medical marijuana. Offerings on its website include medical and scientific information about marijuana, booklets on specific medical conditions treated by marijuana, a history of medical marijuana, press releases, local resources, online discussion forums, and links to allied organizations. ASA also maintains a presence on Facebook, YouTube, and Twitter.

Center for Medicinal Cannabis Research (CMCR)
University of California, San Diego
Department of Psychiatry
220 Dickinson St., Ste. B, MC8231
San Diego, CA 92103-8231
(619) 543-5024
fax: (619) 543-1235
e-mail: cmcr@ucsd.edu
website: www.cmcr.ucsd.edu

The purpose of the University of California's CMCR is to coordinate rigorous scientific studies to assess the safety and efficacy of marijuana and marijuana compounds for treating medical conditions. The CMCR coordinates and supports marijuana research throughout the state of California. Its website offers links to scientific publications about medical marijuana, information on clinical trials (in the FAQ section), and links to news articles discussing the topic. Of particular note are the reports *Marijuana as Medicine?: The Science Beyond the Controversy, Marijuana and Medicine: Assessing the Science*

Base, and CMCR *Legislative Report*, all of which are available for download.

Common Sense for Drug Policy (CSDP)
1377-C Spencer Ave., Lancaster, PA 17603
(717) 299-0600
fax: (717) 393-4953
e-mail: info@csdp.org
website: www.csdp.org

CSDP is dedicated to reforming drug policy and expanding harm reduction. It disseminates information; comments on existing laws, policies, and practices; and provides assistance to individuals and organizations. In addition to advocating the regulation of marijuana in a manner similar to the regulation of alcohol, CSDP favors decriminalizing the use of hard drugs and providing them only through prescription. Its website's medical marijuana section (www.medicalmj.org/) includes medical marijuana news updates and medical marijuana facts.

Drug Free America Foundation (DFAF)
5999 Central Ave., Ste. 301
Saint Petersburg, FL 33710
(727) 828-0211
fax: (727) 828-0212
e-mail: webmaster@dfaf.org
website: www.dfaf.org

The DFAF is a nongovernmental drug prevention and policy organization committed to developing, promoting, and sustaining global strategies, policies, and laws that will reduce illegal drug use, drug addiction, and drug-related injuries and deaths. Its reference collection contains more than twenty-one hundred books and other media chronicling the rise of the drug culture and current drug policy issues. It opposes the use of medical marijuana and favors the war on drugs. Its website contains many articles defending current policy, including student drug testing.

Of particular note is the section on marijuana (www.dfaf.org /questions-answers/marijuana/), which includes information on medical marijuana.

Drug Policy Alliance
131 West, Thirty-Third St., 15th Fl.
New York, NY 10001
(212) 613-8020
fax: (212) 613-8021
e-mail: nyc@drugpolicy.org
website: www.drugpolicy.org

The Drug Policy Alliance believes in the sovereignty of individuals over their own minds and bodies. Its position is that people should be punished for crimes committed against others, but not for using marijuana or other drugs as a personal choice. The alliance, an independent nonprofit organization, supports and publicizes alternatives to current US policies on illegal drugs, including marijuana. To keep Americans informed, the Drug Policy Alliance compiles newspaper articles on drug legalization issues and distributes legislative updates. Its website features a blog and the *Ally* newsletter. Of particular note is the website's section on medical marijuana (www.drugpolicy.org /medical-marijuana), which includes a Resources section and an Activist Toolkit.

Law Enforcement Against Prohibition (LEAP)
121 Mystic Ave., Stes. 7–9
Medford, MA 02155
(781) 393-6985
fax: (781) 393-2964
e-mail: info@leap.cc
website: www.leap.cc

LEAP is a nonprofit educational organization founded by police officers. Its mission is to reduce the multitude of unintended harmful consequences resulting from fighting the war on drugs. Its website contains many articles and multimedia presentations explaining why it believes legalizing drugs would be a more effective way of reducing the crime, disease, and addiction drugs cause. Publications offered on the LEAP website include *End Prohibition Now!*, *Why I Want All Drugs Legalized*, and *Ending the Drug War: A Dream Deferred*. Other offerings include videos, a blog, the *LEAP Newsletter*, and links to LEAP feeds on Facebook, Twitter, YouTube, and Myspace. Searching for *medical marijuana* on LEAP's website returns over a hundred hits.

Marijuana Policy Project (MPP)
236 Massachusetts Ave. NE, Ste. 400
Washington, DC 20002
(202) 462-5747
e-mail: info@mpp.org
website: www.mpp.org

MPP develops and promotes policies to minimize the harm associated with marijuana laws. The project increases public awareness through speaking engagements, educational seminars, and the mass media. Briefing papers and news articles, as well as the quarterly *MPP Report*, can be accessed on its website. The website's section on medical marijuana (www .mpp.org/issues/medical-marijuana/) includes headings such as Medical Marijuana Briefing Paper, Key Aspects of State and D.C. Medical Marijuana Laws, Effective Arguments for Medical Marijuana Advocates, and Medical Marijuana Endorsements and Statements of Support, as well as links to reports and studies, including *Marijuana Arrests in the United States, 2007* and *Revenue & Taxes from Oakland's Cannabis Economy: Report to Measure Z Oversight Committee*.

Multidisciplinary Association for Psychedelic Studies (MAPS)
309 Cedar St. #2323
Santa Cruz, CA 95060
(831) 429-6362
fax: (831) 429-6370
e-mail: askmaps@maps.org
website: http://maps.org

MAPS is a nonprofit research and educational organization that aims to educate the public about the risks and benefits of marijuana and psychedelics and to develop those substances into prescription medicines. It publishes an e-mail newsletter and the triannual magazine *MAPS Bulletin*, the entire archives of which are available online. Its website includes research papers, free psychedelic literature, and audio and video material. Of particular note is its website's section on medical marijuana research (www .maps.org/research/mmj/). Many articles related to medical marijuana can be found on the MAPS website, including "Making the Case for Medical Marijuana: A Legal Perspective," "Obama's Multi-Agency War on Medical Marijuana," and "NIDA Blocks Medical Marijuana Research." MAPS also hosts a moderated discussion forum via e-mail.

National Center on Addiction and Substance Abuse at Columbia University (CASAColumbia)
633 Third Ave., 19th Fl.
New York, NY 10017-6706
(212) 841-5200
website: www.casacolumbia.org

CASAColumbia is a private nonprofit organization that works to educate the public about the hazards of chemical dependency. The organization supports treatment as the best way to reduce chemical dependency and produces numerous publications describing the harmful effects of addiction to marijuana, alcohol, and other drugs, as well as effective ways to address the problem of substance abuse. Publications available on its website include *Non-Medical Marijuana III: Rite of Passage or Russian Roulette?*, *The Importance of Family Dinners VII*, and *National Survey of American Attitudes on Substance Abuse XVII: Teens*. Its website also features videos and the quarterly *CASA Inside* newsletter.

National Institute on Drug Abuse (NIDA)
Office of Science Policy and Communications, Public Information and Liaison Branch
6001 Executive Blvd., Rm. 5213, MSC 9561

Bethesda, MD 20892-9561
(301) 443-1124
e-mail: information@nida.nih.gov
website: www.drugabuse.gov

NIDA is one of the National Institutes of Health, a component of the US Department of Health and Human Services. NIDA supports and conducts research on drug abuse to improve addiction prevention, treatment, and policy efforts. It is dedicated to understanding how drugs of abuse affect the brain and behavior, and it works to rapidly disseminate new information to policy makers, drug abuse counselors, and the general public. It publishes the *NIDA Notes* and *What's New at NIDA?* newsletters; DrugFacts fact sheets, such as *Is Marijuana Medicine?* and *Spice (Synthetic Marijuana)*; and a variety of other publications, including *Seeking Drug Abuse Treatment: Know What to Ask*, *Marijuana: Facts for Teens*, and *Marijuana Abuse*. The website also offers videos, podcasts, e-books, and a section on related topics such as addiction science, drug testing, prevention research, and trends and statistics. Of particular note is the NIDA for Teens section (http://teens.drugabuse.gov/).

National Organization for the Reform of
Marijuana Laws (NORML)
1600 K St. NW, Mezzanine Level
Washington, DC 20006-2832
(202) 483-5500
fax: (202) 483-0057
e-mail: norml@norml.org
website: www.norml.org

Since its founding in 1970, NORML has provided a voice in the public policy debate for those Americans who oppose marijuana prohibition and favor an end to the practice of arresting marijuana users. A nonprofit public interest advocacy group, NORML represents the interests of the tens of millions of Americans who use marijuana. The organization supports the right of adults to use marijuana responsibly for both personal and medical purposes and believes that all penalties should be eliminated for responsible use. Further, NORML believes that a legally regulated market should be established where consumers can buy marijuana in a safe and secure environment. Its website features an extensive section on medical use of marijuana (http://norml.org/marijuana/medical), a blog, the NORML newsletter, news releases, an audio and video section, and a library of information such as the publications "Driving and Marijuana," "Health Reports," and "Medical Marijuana Reports."

Office of National Drug Control Policy (ONDCP)
Drug Policy Information Clearinghouse
PO Box 6000
Rockville, MD 20849-6000
(800) 666-3332
fax: (301) 519-5212
e-mail: ondcp@ncjrs.org
website: www.whitehouse.gov/ondcp

The ONDCP is responsible for formulating the federal government's national drug strategy and the president's antidrug policy, as well as coordinating the federal agencies responsible for stopping drug trafficking. It has launched drug prevention programs, including the National Youth Anti-Drug Media Campaign and Above the Influence. The ONDCP's website features fact sheets such as *Marijuana: Know the Facts, Marijuana Legalization*, and *Synthetic Marijuana*, as well as a blog, news releases, and information on drug treatment and recovery. Of particular note is the ONDCP's Marijuana Resource Center (www.whitehouse.gov/ondcp/marijuanainfo), which includes sections such as Marijuana FAQ, Federal Laws Related to Marijuana, and State Laws Related to Marijuana.

The Partnership at Drugfree.org
352 Park Ave. South, 9th Fl.
New York, NY 10174
(212) 922-1560

fax: (212) 922-1570
website: www.drugfree.org/

The Partnership at Drugfree.org, previously known as The Partnership for a Drug-Free America, is a nonprofit organization that utilizes the media to reduce demand for illicit drugs in America. Best known for its national antidrug advertising campaign, the partnership works to educate children about the dangers of marijuana and other drugs and prevent drug use among youths. It produces the *Partnership Newsletter*, annual reports, and monthly press releases about current events with which the partnership is involved. Searching for *medical marijuana* on its website yields many articles on the topic, such as "Communities Weigh Impact of Medical Marijuana Report," "Commentary: Clearing the Smoke on Medical Marijuana (Parts I & II)," "Is Marijuana Medicine?," and "Study Finds No Link Between Medical Marijuana Dispensaries and Increased Crime."

The Substance Abuse and Mental Health Services Administration (SAMHSA)
1 Choke Cherry Rd.
Rockville, MD 20857
(877) 726-4727
fax: (240) 221-4292
e-mail: samhsainfo@samhsa.hhs.gov
website: www.samhsa.gov

The mission of SAMHSA is to reduce the impact of substance abuse (including marijuana abuse) and mental illness on America's communities. It aims to help create communities where individuals, families, schools, faith-based organizations, and workplaces take action to promote emotional health and reduce the likelihood of substance abuse, mental illness, and suicide. Publications available on its website include *The NSDUH Report: Marijuana Use and Perceived Risk of Use Among Adolescents: 2002 to 2007*, *The NSDUH Report: How Youths Obtain Marijuana*, *The NSDUH Report: Age at First Use of Marijuana and Past Year Serious Mental Illness*, and *Tips for Teens: The Truth About Marijuana*. Under the Substances heading on the main page, click on "Marijuana" to see a list of several dozen downloadable reports containing information on the topic.

US Drug Enforcement Administration (DEA)
Attn: Office of Diversion Control
8701 Morrissette Dr.
Springfield, VA 22152
(202) 307-1000
website: www.justice.gov/dea

The DEA is the federal agency charged with enforcing the nation's drug laws and regulations. It coordinates the activities of federal, state, and local agencies and works with foreign governments to reduce the availability of illicit drugs in the United States. The DEA publishes the biannual *Microgram Journal* and the monthly *Microgram Bulletin*. Numerous DEA publications are available on its website, including *The DEA Position on Marijuana* and *Get It Straight— The Facts About Drugs Student Guide (2011)*. Drug fact sheets, videos, and a section specifically for teens (www.justthinktwice.com/) can also be found on its website.

BIBLIOGRAPHY

Books

Joan Bello, *The Benefits of Marijuana: Physical, Psychological and Spiritual*. Final ed. Boca Raton, FL: Lifeservices, 2010.

Martin Booth, *Cannabis: A History*. New York: Picador, 2005.

Greg Campbell, *Pot, Inc.: Inside Medical Marijuana, America's Most Outlaw Industry*. New York: Sterling, 2012.

Jonathan P. Caulkins, Angela Hawken, Beau Kilmer, and Mark A.R. Kleiman, *Marijuana Legalization: What Everyone Needs to Know*. New York: Oxford University Press, 2012.

Mitch Earleywine, *Understanding Marijuana: A New Look at the Scientific Evidence*. New York: Oxford University Press, 2005.

David Emmett and Graeme Nice, *What You Need to Know About Cannabis: Understanding the Facts*. London: Jessica Kingsley, 2009.

Doug Fine, *Too High to Fail: Cannabis and the New Green Economic Revolution*. New York: Gotham, 2012.

Steve Fox, Paul Armentano, and Mason Tvert, *Marijuana Is Safer: So Why Are We Driving People to Drink?* White River Junction, VT: Chelsea Green, 2009.

Matthew Gavin Frank, *Pot Farm*. Lincoln: University of Nebraska Press, 2012.

John Geluardi, Cannabiz: *The Explosive Rise of the Medical Marijuana Industry*. Sausalito, CA: PoliPoint, 2010.

Julie Holland, *The Pot Book: A Complete Guide to Cannabis; Its Role in Medicine, Politics, Science, and Culture*. Rochester, VT: Park Street, 2010.

Martin A. Lee, *Smoke Signals: A Social History of Marijuana—Medical, Recreational and Scientific*. New York: Scribner, 2012.

Mickey Martin, Ed Rosenthal, and Gregory T. Carter, *Medical Marijuana 101*. Oakland, CA: Quick American Archives, 2011.

David Nutt, *Drugs Without the Hot Air: Minimising the Harms of Legal and Illegal Drugs*. Cambridge: UIT Cambridge, 2012.

Trish Regan, *Joint Ventures: Inside America's Almost Legal Marijuana Industry*. Hoboken, NJ: Wiley, 2011.

Winifred Rosen and Andrew T. Weil, *From Chocolate to Morphine: Everything You Need to Know About Mind-Altering Drugs*. New York: Mariner, 2004.

Mark Haskell Smith, *Heart of Dankness: Underground Botanists, Outlaw Farmers, and the Race for the Cannabis Cup*. New York: Broadway, 2012.

Clint Werner, *Marijuana: Gateway to Health; How Cannabis Protects Us from Cancer and Alzheimer's Disease*. San Francisco: Dachstar, 2011.

Periodicals and Internet Sources

Paul Armentano, "Medical Marijuana Has Come of Age: Celebrating the 10th Anniversary of a Landmark Scientific Study," *Reason*, March 17, 2009.

Paul Armentano, David G. Evans, and Kevin A. Sabet, "3 Views on Whether States Should Legalize Marijuana," *Christian Science Monitor*, September 10, 2012. www.csmonitor.com /Commentary/One-Minute-Debate/2012/0910/3-views-on -whether-states-should-legalize-marijuana/Yes-Follow-the -model-of-tobacco-regulation.-Its-use-is-at-a-historic-low.

Sara Calabro, "Medical Marijuana for Chronic Pain," *Everyday Health*, April 4, 2011. www.everydayhealth.com/pain-manage ment/medical-marijuana-for-chronic-pain.aspx.

Rebecca Richman Cohen, "The Fight over Medical Marijuana," *New York Times*, November 7, 2012. www.nytimes.com /2012/11/08/opinion/the-fight-over-medical-marijuana.html? _r=1&.

Chelsea Conaboy, "Pot Perceptions: Some Worry That Legalizing Marijuana Could Drive Use Among Teens, Leading to Long-Term Damage," Boston.com, September 23, 2012. www .boston.com/lifestyle/health/2012/09/23/does-approving-the -use-medical-marijuana-cause-teens-see-the-drug-safe-for -recreational-use/FwfPPTHjkl7OCkknJcy0sN/story.html.

John Diaz, "Medical Marijuana—Lost in the Haze of State Law," SF Gate, October 31, 2011. www.sfgate.com/default/article /Medical-marijuana-lost-in-the-haze-of-state-law-2325997.php.

Tony Dokoupil, "The New Pot Barons: Businessmen Bank on Marijuana," The Daily Beast, October 22, 2012. www.the dailybeast.com/newsweek/2012/10/21/will-pot-barons-cash-in -on-legalization.html.

David Downs, "What the Funk? Terpenes Take Off in Labs, Drug Companies, and Dispensaries," *East Bay Express* (Alameda and Contra Costa Counties, CA), January 24, 2012. www .eastbayexpress.com/LegalizationNation/archives/2012/01/24 /what-the-funk-terpenes-take-off-in-labs-drug-companies-and -dispensaries.

Andrew Ferguson, "The United States of Amerijuana," *Time*, November 11, 2010. www.time.com/time/magazine/article /0,9171,2030925,00.html.

David Freed, "California's Medical Marijuana Morass," *Pacific Standard*, January 3, 2012. www.psmag.com/legal-affairs /californias-medical-marijuana-morass-38772/.

Emily Gibson, "The Unintended Consequences of Medical Marijuana," KevinMD.com, June 10, 2011. www.kevinmd.com /blog/2011/06/unintended-consequences-medical-marijuana .html.

Ed Gogek, "A Bad Trip for Democrats," *New York Times*, November 7, 2012. www.nytimes.com/2012/11/08/opinion /a-bad-trip-for-democrats.html.

James Hamblin, "Study: Medical Marijuana Becomes Party Doobies for Kids," *The Atlantic*, August 9, 2012. www.the

atlantic.com/health/archive/2012/08/study-medical-marijuana -becomes-party-doobies-for-kids/260891/.

Peter Hecht, "Research Backs Up Claims of Medical Marijuana's Benefits," *The Sacramento Bee*, July 12, 2012. www.sacbee .com/2012/07/12/4625608/california-pot-research-backs.html.

Charles Lane, "Medical Marijuana Is an Insult to Our Intelligence," *Washington Post*, October 20, 2009. http://voices.washington post.com/postpartisan/2009/10/medical_marijuana_is_an _insult.html.

Marie Myung-Ok Lee, "My Mother-in-Law's One High Day," *New York Times*, December 9, 2011. www.nytimes.com/2011/12/10 /opinion/medical-marijuana-and-the-memory-of-one-high-day .html.

Sharon Letts, "Cannabis: Self-Medicating and Wellness," Toke of the Town, June 15, 2012. www.tokeofthetown.com/2012/06 /cannabis_self-medicating_and_wellness.php.

Kristy Naylor Lund, "Recreational Drug to Cancer Solution," *Whole Life Times*, October 16, 2010. www.wholelifemagazine .com/blog/?p=1321.

Jonathan Martin, "Medical Marijuana: 'Medibles' Industry Thrives, Lacks Safety Regulations," *Seattle Times*, October 7, 2012. http://seattletimes.com/html/localnews/2019372300 _medibles08m.html.

Annalee Newitz, "What Cannabis Actually Does to Your Brain," io9, April 20, 2012. http://io9.com/5903837/what-cannabis -actually-does-to-your-brain.

Henry Percy, "Medical Marijuana and Peer Review Science," *American Thinker*, September 29, 2010. www.americanthinker .com/blog/2010/09/medical_marijuana_and_peer_rev.html.

Gustin L. Reichbach, "A Judge's Plea for Pot," *New York Times*, May 16, 2012. www.nytimes.com/2012/05/17/opinion/a-judges -plea-for-medical-marijuana.html?_r=0.

Lee Romney, "On the Frontier of Medical Pot to Treat Boy's Epilepsy," *Los Angeles Times*, September 13, 2012.

www.latimes.com/news/local/la-me-customized-marijua
na-20120914,0,7012444.story.

John Schwarz, "Obama, What About 'Free and Open Scientific
Inquiry' for Medical Marijuana?," *Huffington Post*, November
1, 2012. www.huffingtonpost.com/dr-john-schwarz/medical
- marijuana_b_2050358.html.

Nathan Seppa, "Not Just a High: Scientists Test Medicinal
Marijuana Against MS, Inflammation and Cancer," Science
News, June 19, 2010. www.sciencenews.org/view/feature
/id/59872/title/Not just_a_high.

Jacob Sullum, "Anti-pot Psychiatrist: Democrats, as Paternalistic
Control Freaks, Must Oppose Medical Marijuana," *Reason*,
November 8, 2012. http://reason.com/blog/2012/11/08/anti
-pot-psychiatrist-democrats-as-pater.

Maia Szalavitz, "The Link Between Marijuana and Schizophrenia,"
Time, July 21, 2010. www.time.com/time/health/arti
cle/0,8599,2005559,00.html.

Tamar Todd, "Why I Want a Medical Marijuana Dispensary Near
My Children's School," *Huffington Post*, May 7, 2012. www
.huffingtonpost.com/tamar-todd/why-i-want-a-medical-mari
juana-dispensary-near-school_b_1497917.html.

Jeff vonKaenel, "Is the War on Drugs a War on Jobs?: California's
Search for a Sane Drug Policy," *Sacramento News & Review*,
October 27, 2011. www.newsreview.com/sacramento/is-the
-war-on- drugs/content?oid=4247012.

Allyson Weller, "Toddler Is One of Youngest Medical Marijuana
Patients in Montana," KBZK, February 22, 2011. www.kbzk
.com/news/toddler-is-one-of-youngest-medical-marijuana
-patients-in-montana/.

Controlled Substances Act (1970), 54, 55
marijuana as Schedule 1 drug under, 15, 58
marijuana should be rescheduled under, 57
Craker, Lyle, 52

D
DEA. *See* Drug Enforcement Administration, US
Deaths
annual hospital-related, from MRSA infections, 24
overdose, due to opioids *vs.* marijuana, 36
Doblin, Rick, 51
Dronabinol, effectiveness of, *vs.* placebo, 61
Drug and Alcohol Dependence (journal), 40
Drug Enforcement Administration, US (DEA), 25, 49, 50, 52, 57
on marijuana research, 30–31
Drug Policy Alliance, 16
Drug Policy Foundation, 16
Drugs, illicit
emergency room visits involving, by age and drug, 31
federal classification of, 15

E
Emergency room visits, involving illicit drugs, by age and drug, 31

Europe, drug laws in, 16–18
European Movement for the Normalization of Drug Policy, 16

F
FDA. *See* Food and Drug Administration, US
Finley, Nolan, 67
Food and Drug Administration, US (FDA), 26, 32, 49, 59
on raw marijuana, 59
Fox, Steve, 19

G
Gibson, Emily, 5, 8
Glaucoma, 13, 20
Gonzales v. Raich (2005), 26
Gregoire, Chris, 59
Griffiths, Heather M., 10
Gust, Stephen, 49–50
Guzman, Manuel, 24

H
Harm Reduction Journal, 41
HIV disease, 20, 22, 50
Holland, Julie, 8

I
INCB (International Narcotics Control Board), 26–27
Institute of Medicine (IOM), 29–30, 51, 59
International Anti-Prohibition League, 16